POTTER V. SHRACKLE

and

THE SHRACKLE CONSTRUCTION COMPANY

Fifth Edition

POTTER V. SHRACKLE

and

THE SHRACKLE CONSTRUCTION COMPANY

Fifth Edition

KENNETH S. BROUN

Henry Brandis Professor of Law
University of North Carolina
School of Law

FRANK D. ROTHSCHILD

Attorney at Law
Kilauea, Hawaii

Revision by Kenneth S. Broun and Frank D. Rothschild based upon the original file
created by Kenneth S. Broun as revised by James H. Seckinger

THE NATIONAL INSTITUTE FOR TRIAL ADVOCACY

©1977, 1979, 1981, 1983, 1986, 1990, 1992, 1999, 2002, 2004
by the National Institute for Trial Advocacy

Broun, Kenneth S. and Frank D. Rothschild, *Potter v. Shrackle and the Shrackle Construction Company,* 5th ed. (NITA, 2004).

FBA801-7

3/04

CONTENTS

Exhibits

ACKNOWLEDGMENTS

The authors would like to thank the following for their assistance in the creation of the photographs and video clips that come with this file: Craig Gilbert, general contractor (Charles Shrackle); Bobby Dudley, former contractor and recent law school graduate (Jeffrey Potter); Bob Bissenette, commercial painter (James Marshall); Courtney Haas, realtor and yoga instructor (Cheryl Tobias); and especially Anne Slifkin, attorney and mediator, whose portrayal of Kathy Potter in the original version of this file (c. 1976) became part of NITA lore.

We are also deeply indebted to Juan Gonzalez III, Principal, and Jaime Jue, Senior Associate, in the Forensic department of KPMG LLP for their outstanding work in upgrading and enriching the experts portion of this file, including the reports and tables of Dr. Glenn and Dr. Buchanan, the Dyer memorandum, and other related materials.

INTRODUCTION

This is a wrongful death action brought in Nita state court by Jeffrey T. Potter, as administrator of the estate of his deceased wife, Katherine, and in his own behalf, against Charles T. Shrackle and the Shrackle Construction Company. Potter claims that Shrackle negligently drove the company's pickup, striking Katherine Potter as she was crossing the street, causing her death. Potter claims that Shrackle was acting in the course of the Shrackle Construction Company's business at the time of the accident.

Shrackle admits striking Mrs. Potter, but claims that she was crossing in the middle of the street, rather than in the pedestrian crosswalk, and that she did not look before entering the street in the path of Mr. Shrackle's truck. Defendants deny that Shrackle was negligent and allege contributory negligence on the part of the deceased, Mrs. Potter.

The applicable law is contained in the proposed jury instructions set forth at the end of the file.

SPECIAL INSTRUCTIONS FOR USE AS A FULL TRIAL

Issues for Trial

This case file may be used for a full trial on the issue of liability only or on the issues of both liability and damages. If used solely for the issue of liability, the proposed jury instructions should be modified accordingly by the deletion of instructions 16 and 17.

Witnesses

For the plaintiff:

> Officer Michael Young
> Marilyn Kelly
> James Marshall
> Jeffrey Potter
> Daniel Sloan
> Robert Glenn

For the defendant:

> Charles Shrackle
> Alice Mallory
> Victoria Williams
> Juanita Williams
> Benjamin Grimson
> Elizabeth Buchanan

A party need not call all of the persons listed as its witnesses. Any or all of the witnesses may be called by any party, subject to the limitations below. However, if a witness is to be called by a party other than the one for whom he or she is listed, the party for whom the witness is listed will select and prepare the witness.

Limitation on Witnesses

Each party is limited to four witnesses.

For the plaintiff

> Daniel Sloan's testimony is stipulated. If the trial is on both liability and damages, Dr. Robert Glenn is available to testify and the testimony of James Marshall will be stipulated. If tried on the issue of liability alone, James Marshall is available to testify.

For the defendant:

> The testimony of Benjamin Grimson is stipulated, as well as the information about his subsequent imprisonment. If the trial is on both liability and damages, Elizabeth Buchanan is available to testify, and the testimony of Juanita Williams will be stipulated.

Required Stipulations

Where testimony is stipulated pursuant to the above instructions, the statement or deposition of the witness is admissible and may be impeached by other information in the file.

Defendant submitted a Request for Admissions with regard to the accuracy and authenticity of Exhibits 29, 30, 31, and 32. Plaintiff filed admissions to all four exhibits.

The formula for calculating how many feet per second a vehicle travels is to multiply the miles per hour by 1.47.

Suggested Time Limits for Full Trial

Voir dire	10 minutes per side (5 minutes per attorney when teamed up)
Opening statement	15 minutes per side
Witness examination	100 minutes per side
Closing argument	20 minutes per side

IN THE CIRCUIT COURT OF
DARROW COUNTY, NITA
CIVIL DIVISION

Jeffrey T. Potter, the Administrator of the Estate of Katherine Potter, and Jeffrey T. Potter, individually, 　　　Plaintiffs, v. Charles T. Shrackle and The Shrackle Construction Company, 　　　Defendants.	)))))))))))))))	**Complaint**

Plaintiff, Jeffrey T. Potter, individually and as administrator of the Estate of Katherine Potter, complains against Defendants, Charles T. Shrackle and Shrackle Construction Company as follows:

FIRST CLAIM FOR RELIEF

1. Plaintiff was, and still is, a resident of Darrow County, Nita.

2. Defendant Charles T. Shrackle was, and still is, a resident of Darrow County, Nita, and the Defendant Shrackle Construction Company was, and still is, doing business in Darrow County, Nita.

3. Katherine Potter died on December 4, 2001.

4. Plaintiff and Katherine Potter were married at the time of her death and had been married for twelve years.

5. Plaintiff has been duly appointed the Administrator of Katherine Potter's estate.

6. On November 30, 2001, at about 3:30 P.M., Katherine Potter was walking in an easterly direction across Mattis Avenue at the intersection of Mattis and Kirby Avenues in Nita City, Nita.

7. At this time and place Defendant Charles T. Shrackle was driving a 2001 Toyota pickup truck which struck Katherine Potter, causing her serious injuries and that Katherine Potter died as a result of such injuries on December 4, 2001.

8. The truck driven by Defendant Charles T. Shrackle was owned by the Defendant Shrackle Construction Company, and at the time Katherine Potter was struck by the truck, Charles T. Shrackle was performing duties for and acting on behalf of the Shrackle Construction Company.

9. Defendant Charles T. Shrackle was driving the Toyota pickup truck in a careless, negligent, and reckless manner, and in violation of his duties under Nita Revised Statutes 89-12(4)(2002) to exercise due care to avoid striking the pedestrian Katherine Potter who was then lawfully walking across the street.

10. Defendant Charles T. Shrackle carelessly, negligently, and in violation of Nita Revised Statutes 89-12(4)(2002) failed to keep a proper lookout, to heed the fact that Katherine Potter was crossing the street in the immediate path of his truck, or to take any action to avoid striking Katherine Potter.

11. Defendant Charles T. Shrackle carelessly, negligently, and in violation of Nita Revised Statutes 89-12(4)(2002) failed to give proper warning of the sudden and unexpected approach of his truck either by sounding the horn or giving any other signal or warning.

12. Defendant Charles T. Shrackle's negligence caused Katherine Potter to suffer severe physical and mental pain and suffering from the date such injuries were incurred on November 30, 2001, until her death on December 4, 2001.

13. Defendant Charles T. Shrackle's negligence caused Katherine Potter to incur reasonable expenses for medical, hospital, and surgical care and the loss of wages from the time of the collision until her death, in the sum of $107,800.

14. Defendant Charles T. Shrackle's negligence caused Jeffrey Potter, as personal representative of the Estate of Katherine Potter, to incur reasonable funeral and burial expenses, in the sum of $16,500.

SECOND CLAIM FOR RELIEF

15. Plaintiff re-alleges paragraphs 1 through 11.

16. Defendant Charles T. Shrackle's negligence caused Jeffrey Potter, as the surviving spouse of Katherine Potter, to suffer damages for the loss of:

    (a) The reasonable expected net income of Katherine Potter;

    (b) Services, protection, care, and assistance of Katherine Potter, whether voluntary or obligatory, to Jeffrey Potter;

    (c) Society, companionship, comfort, guidance, kindly offices, and advice of Katherine Potter to Jeffrey Potter.

WHEREFORE, Plaintiff demands judgment against Defendants, jointly and severally, in an amount in excess of $50,000, together with interest thereon and his costs herein, and for such other relief as the Court deems just and proper.

JURY DEMAND

Plaintiff demands a trial by jury in this action.

MADDEN & JAMES

by

William James

Attorneys for Plaintiff
Suite 720, Nita Bank Building
Nita City, Nita 99994
(721) 555-0003

DATED: April 7, 2002

IN THE CIRCUIT COURT OF
DARROW COUNTY, NITA
CIVIL DIVISION

Jeffrey T. Potter, the	)	
Administrator of the Estate	)	
of Katherine Potter, and	)	
Jeffrey T. Potter, individually,	)	
	)	
Plaintiffs,	)	
	)	
v.	)	**Answer**
	)	
Charles T. Shrackle and	)	
Shrackle Construction Company,	)	
	)	
Defendants.	)	

Defendants for their Answer to Plaintiff's Complaint:

1.   Admit the allegations contained in paragraphs 1–5, 7–8.

2.   Admit that on November 30, 2001, at or about 3:30 P.M., Katherine Potter was crossing Mattis Avenue somewhere near the intersection of Kirby and Mattis Avenues. Defendants deny all other allegations in paragraph 6.

3.   Deny the allegations contained in paragraphs 9–14, 16.

FIRST AFFIRMATIVE DEFENSE

4.   Any injuries sustained or suffered by Katherine Potter at the time and place mentioned in the Complaint were caused, in whole or in part, or were contributed to, by the negligence of Katherine Potter and not by any negligence of Charles T. Shrackle.

SECOND AFFIRMATIVE DEFENSE

5.   Katherine Potter violated Nita Revised Statutes 89-12(4)(2002) by failing to cross the street in the marked pedestrian crosswalk, to keep a proper lookout for vehicles using the roadway and to yield the right of way to any such vehicles.

WHEREFORE, Defendants demand that judgment be entered in favor of the Defendants with the costs and disbursements of this action.

PIERCE, JOHNSON & CLARK

by

James Barber

Attorneys for Defendants
Nita National Bank Plaza
Nita City, Nita 99994
(721) 555-6207

DATED: April 16, 2002

SUMMARY OF DEPOSITION OF MARILYN J. KELLY

1 My name is Marilyn J. Kelly. I live at 1910 Elder Lane, Nita City 99992.
2
3 On November 30, 2001, I was driving my car on Mattis Avenue, traveling in a northeasterly
4 direction. I was in the lane of traffic closest to the east side of the street. At approximately 3:20
5 P.M., I was stopped for a red light at the intersection of Mattis and Kirby Avenues. I was first in
6 line and was stopped just south of the crosswalk.
7
8 Just as I stopped, a small boy ran across the street from the west to east and barely avoided
9 being struck by a car making a left turn from Kirby onto Mattis heading south. When he reached
10 the sidewalk, I heard the crossing guard who was standing on the southeast corner of the
11 intersection speak to the boy and say something to the effect that, "You have got to watch for cars."
12
13 Just then I saw a woman with dark hair dressed in a dark jacket with some color on it and a
14 dark skirt on the west side of Mattis Avenue. She was just stepping off the curb and starting to
15 cross the street when I saw her. At that time the woman was walking at a normal gait and was not
16 running. She was definitely in the crosswalk, and I saw her take two or three steps.
17
18 I then glanced back up at the light, and at that time I heard a thud. I looked up and saw the
19 woman flying through the air and then land with arms outstretched on the front of the truck. She
20 then went backward as if doing a backward somersault and fell under the truck. She didn't
21 complete a somersault, but just flew back and landed with her head smashing on the pavement. At
22 that time I thought to myself, "My God, stop, don't run over her again." The truck driver appeared to
23 be looking around immediately after the impact as though looking to see what he had hit.
24
25 The truck stopped at a point approximately forty feet south of the south line of Kirby. At the
26 point where the truck stopped, the woman was almost entirely underneath the truck. I definitely
27 heard the thud before I heard the sound of any brakes shrieking. At the time of the thud the front
28 of the truck was about even with the front of my car and was not completely straightened out
29 from making the left turn.
30
31 The sun at the time of the occurrence was extremely bright and low in the sky, coming from a
32 southwesterly direction. I had to shade my eyes when I looked back to the scene after the truck
33 came to a stop.
34
35 After the truck stopped, a man ran out from the car wash across the street and the driver of
36 the truck got out and went around to the front of the truck. I thought that the guy driving the truck
37 was Charles Shrackle, but I wasn't sure at the time.
38

Potter v. Shrackle Case File

1   I stayed at the scene for a couple of minutes, and then I left and went to my appointment with
2   my firm's accountant in the Lincolnshire Shopping Plaza. My appointment was at 3:30 P.M.
3   Lincolnshire is about a fifteen minute drive from Kirby and Mattis. I was particularly concerned
4   about the time because traffic had been heavy that day as I came up Mattis. The schools were
5   getting out just as I was traveling on Mattis. What ordinarily would be a ten-minute trip for me
6   took me close to twenty-five minutes.
7
8   I am thirty-seven years old. I work as the office manager of a local construction company,
9   Buildit. Although I don't know Charles Shrackle well, I know his business is a competitor of our
10   company. I have met him at some Builder's Association meetings. Frankly, I don't like him
11   much. He has always seemed arrogant—somebody who's always in a hurry to get to the top. It's
12   funny that he is so ambitious, because I don't think his company is doing that well. We took over
13   one school construction job from them a year or so ago when the school district was unhappy
14   with the progress of the work.
15
16   The following morning after I got to work, I read about the accident in the Nita City
17   newspaper. The newspaper article said that the woman was running and was approximately thirty
18   feet south of the crosswalk at the time she was hit by the truck. They got it all wrong. I told my
19   boss, Susannah Bond, about it. Susannah advised me that I should call the police and tell them
20   what I saw. So I called the police and advised them that I had witnessed the accident, and that the
21   woman was in the crosswalk and not running at all.
22
23   Susannah and I then talked about Shrackle some. Susannah told me about Shrackle's
24   problems on the Greenbriar job. She told me there was some possibility we were going to take
25   over that Greenbriar project if Shrackle didn't get his act together.
26
27   I did not know Katherine Potter, nor do I know Jeffrey Potter or anyone else in their family.
28
29   I have read the foregoing and it is a true and accurate transcription of my deposition
30   testimony given on December 12, 2002.
31
32   Signed: *Marilyn J. Kelly*   Date: 12/12/2002
33   Marilyn J. Kelly
34
35   Subscribed and sworn to before me this 12th day of December, 2002.
36
37   *Lucy Madison*
38   Lucy Madison
39   Notary
40

SUMMARY OF DEPOSITION OF JUANITA WILLIAMS

1   My name is Juanita Williams. I live at 1010 West Kirby, Unit 15, in Nita City. I work part-
2 time as a secretary. I am a single mother with two children, Victoria, age ten and Joshua, age three.
3
4   On November 30, 2001, at approximately 3:30 P.M. I was at the corner of Kirby and Mattis.
5 I was stopped on Kirby Avenue, west of the intersection, facing east getting ready for the light to
6 change to green. I had just picked up Victoria at Senn School and was driving to pick up Josh at his
7 day care.
8
9   A man in a pickup truck was in the lefthand lane of westbound Kirby on the opposite side
10 of the intersection with his left turn signal on as he was waiting to turn southwest on Mattis. It
11 looked like he was talking on his cell phone or he may have simply had his hand up to his ear. The
12 light changed to green, he waited until I had passed, and with the light still green he turned southwest
13 on Mattis. The pickup truck took the turn a little fast, maybe at about twenty miles an hour. He sort
14 of rolled through the intersection and then picked up speed.
15
16   I actually didn't see him hit the dark-haired woman, who I later found out was Mrs.
17 Potter, but he could not have been going fast because I was only a few feet from the intersection
18 when my daughter said, "Mom, someone was just hit." We immediately turned around and went
19 back to the accident.
20
21   When we went back to the intersection and parked at the White Castle, I saw the dark-haired
22 woman lying underneath the pickup truck. I saw that funny Superman logo on the truck.
23
24   I didn't know Mrs. Potter or anyone in her family. I don't know Charles Shrackle and I
25 never heard of Shrackle Construction Company until the time of the accident.
26
27   I have read the foregoing and it is a true and accurate transcription of my deposition
28 testimony given on December 12, 2002.
29
30
31 Signed _Juanita Williams_   Date: ___12/12/2002___
32   Juanita Williams
33
34 Signed and sworn to before me this 12th day of December, 2002.
35
36 _Joseph Lucey_
37 Joseph Lucey
38 Notary

SUMMARY OF DEPOSITION OF VICTORIA WILLIAMS

1   My name is Vicky Williams and I am ten years old. I live at 1010 W. Kirby Avenue in Nita
2   City with my mom and my brother, Joshua. Joshua is three.
3
4   My mom was driving me home from school on November 30, 2001. She always picks me up. I
5   was in the back seat in the car. I don't remember if I had my seat belt on but I usually do.
6   I think was about 3:30 in the afternoon when the accident happened.
7
8   We were headed toward town on Kirby Avenue. On the map you showed me that would be
9   going east. (Exhibit 3) We stopped for a light where Kirby crosses Mattis near the White Castle.
10 There was a man in a truck coming towards us on the opposite side of the intersection getting ready
11 to make a left turn onto Mattis. I was looking at some of my school friends who were on the
12 sidewalk in front of the tire store. There were three or four of them. I waved and smiled at my
13 friends trying to get their attention.
14
15 Then my mom started to move and crossed the intersection. The man in the truck took his turn
16 after we passed him. I saw him because I was looking towards my friends. A lady with black or
17 brown hair I think was standing on the center strip on Mattis a little down from the crosswalk. She
18 was facing towards my friends with her back to us. She just stepped right off the center strip right
19 in front of the truck. I saw the truck hit her and her purse went flying into the air. The truck
20 screeched his brakes and stopped. You're right that the sun was a little in my eyes but I could see
21 what happened to the lady. I probably just put my hand up to my forehead so I could see my friends
22 even though the sun was out, but I really don't remember. I know I could see what I told you about.
23
24 I told my mom what happened, that I thought the lady was hit by the truck, and she turned
25 around and we went back and parked in the White Castle parking lot. I saw the lady that got hit
26 lying underneath the truck. It was pretty scary.

Page 14

1. Q.   Where was the woman when you first saw her?

2. A.   She was down the crosswalk on Mattis.

3. Q.   Do you mean south of the crosswalk?

4. A.   I'm not too good with directions. She was away from Kirby Street.

5. Q.   How many feet was she away from Kirby?

Potter v. Shrackle Case File

6. A.   I'm not too good with guessing feet. I would say maybe twenty feet.

7. Q.   Could it have been less?

8. A.   Maybe, but I'd say about twenty. Fifteen or twenty.

9. Q.   How wide is Mattis Avenue at that point?

10. A.   Gee, I don't know. Probably a couple of hundred feet wide.

11 I looked at the map and picture that you called Exhibit 17 and it shows about where we were
12 and what I could see when I first saw the lady standing on the center strip. The map and picture
13 that you called Exhibit 18 shows about where we were when I saw the purse flying in the air.
14
15 I have read the foregoing and it is a true and accurate transcription of my deposition
16 testimony given on December 12, 2002.
17
18
19
20 Signed *Victoria Williams*   Date: 12/12/2002
21   Victoria Williams
22
23
24 Signed and sworn to before me this 12th day of December, 2002.
25
26
27 *Joseph Lucey*
28 Joseph Lucey
29 Notary
30
31
32
33
34
35
36
37
38
39

SUMMARY OF DEPOSITION OF ALICE MALLORY

1   My name is Alice Mallory. I am forty-seven years old. I am married and have two
2   children, both of whom are in high school. I work part-time as a school crossing guard at the
3   corner of Mattis and Kirby. I have done that work for about two years. I work both in the
4   morning and in the afternoon at that corner.
5
6   On the afternoon of November 30, 2001, I was working on the southwest corner of the
7   intersection. At about 3:25, I crossed over to the southeast corner of the street by the White
8   Castle to reprimand a small boy who had not heeded my warning to stop. He had run out in front
9   of some cars but luckily wasn't hurt. I was extremely upset by the incident. The boy could have
10 been killed. It would be the worst thing I could imagine—a child being killed while I was the
11 guard. Exhibit 9 shows where I started out in the foreground, and also where I was in front of the
12 White Castle when I saw Mrs. Potter across the street. As I knelt to talk to him, I saw over his
13 head a woman, who I later learned was Mrs. Katherine Potter, cross the street from west to east
14 in the crosswalk. I can't remember what she was wearing or much about her, but I remember that
15 she had dark hair.
16
17 When she reached the median, she suddenly turned south and began to walk south on the
18 median strip. I then looked down to continue talking to the boy. I then heard a thump and looked
19 up instantly. I saw Mrs. Potter being carried on the hood of a pickup truck about thirty feet south
20 of the crosswalk. The truck stopped about twenty feet later. I ran over to see if I could help, but
21 others got there before me, so I returned to looking after the children.
22
23 At the time I was watching Mrs. Potter, I was also watching children on the other corner. I
24 was really concerned that one of them would cross the street in a dangerous way. However, I did
25 see clearly all that I have said here. I did not come forward as a witness originally because I was
26 upset and didn't want my story to hurt Mrs. Potter or her family. I was finally contacted by the
27 defendant's lawyer and told her what I saw.
28
29 Three weeks after this incident, just before Christmas, I resigned my position as a school
30 crossing guard. The tension of looking after children was too much for me. I guess I was also
31 affected by Mrs. Potter's accident and death.
32
33 Also, my eyesight has become worse. I have a degenerative eye condition that will get
34 progressively worse as I age. I still see pretty well with corrective lenses and feel that I could
35 have kept on as a guard for a little longer. However, the pressure of concern for the children and
36 the trauma of the accident caused me to quit early.
37
38

1   Yes, I was wearing my corrective lenses at the time of the accident. My sight is normal with

2   those lenses although there are some limits to my peripheral vision. I have what is known as

3   primary open-angle glaucoma. It was undiagnosed for a long time and hadn't been diagnosed at

4   the time of the accident. They discovered that my central vision is fine, but that I have some

5   weakening peripheral vision. It was just starting to be a problem at the time of the accident. I had

6   surgery about two months ago that my doctor says will correct most of the problem.

7

8   I have read the foregoing and it is a true and accurate transcription of my deposition

9   testimony given on December 13, 2002.

10

11

12   Signed   _Alice Mallory_   Date: _December 13, 2002_

13   Alice Mallory

14

15   Signed and sworn to before me this 13th day of December, 2002.

16

17

18   _Able Ames_

19   Able Ames

20   Notary

21

22

23

24

25

26

27

28

29

30

31

32

33

34

35

36

37

38

39

40

SUMMARY OF DEPOSITION OF BENJAMIN GRIMSON

1   My name is Benjamin Grimson. I just turned nineteen years old. I am presently in prison at
2 Allenwood Prison in Allenwood, Nita.
3
4   On November 30 last year, I was cruising down Mattis in this Camry when I decided to stop
5 for a burger and fries at the White Castle on Kirby. My buddy, Eddie, works there and he waited
6 on me at the drive-through after I placed my order. As I was heading away from the pay booth, I
7 heard a loud thump and when I looked over there was this lady flying from the air on the front of
8 a truck. I yelled, "Holy shit, somebody smashed up that lady." When I saw her she was in mid-
9 air. At that point, I'd say she was about ten feet south of the crosswalk. The truck must have
10 carried her another thirty-five feet or so. When I saw the truck carrying her, it looked like it was
11 still going pretty fast, maybe twenty miles an hour. The truck stopped and the driver got out of
12 the truck. He said something but I couldn't hear what it was. A bunch of people ran over to her. I
13 decided there wasn't anything I could do so I got my burger and drink and got out. There wasn't
14 anybody behind me, so I backed up and went out the Kirby Street entrance.
15
16   The picture that says Exhibit 19 shows the drive-through lane at the White Castle. Exhibits
17 20 and 21 show what you can see of Mattis Avenue from further down the drive-through lane.
18 That's where I was when I saw this lady.
19
20   Eddie must have told somebody I had been at the drive-through window when the accident
21 occurred. He also told you where to find me.
22
23   On February 25, 2002, I was arrested for grand larceny automobile. I was charged as an
24 adult with the theft of several cars, including the 1999 Toyota Camry I was driving when I saw
25 the accident. The car belonged to one of the teachers at the high school I attended. I am now
26 serving a sentence of two years at Allenwood, which is a minimum security Nita prison.
27
28   I have read the foregoing and it is a true and accurate transcription of my deposition
29 testimony given on December 16, 2002.
30
31 Signed _____   Date ___December 16, 2002___
32   Benjamin Grimson
33
34 Subscribed and sworn to before me this 16th day of December, 2002.
35
36 _____
37 Tracy Williams
38 Notary

SUMMARY OF DEPOSITION OF MICHAEL YOUNG

[handwritten: ✱check most recent assignments]

1   I am Michael Young. I am a police officer for the Nita Police Department and have been on

2   the police force for seven years. My duties have consisted largely of general patrol duty during

3   that time. I was assigned to patrol duty on November 30, 2001. *[handwritten: 11/30/2001 → Date of accident]*

4

5   The afternoon of November 30 was clear, the sun was shining. The pavement was dry. There

6   had not been rain for several days. Exhibit 25 is a printout from the Nita City Weather Bureau's

7   Web site that I printed out for that day. I remember later, at the scene of the accident, that I

8   thought that the sun was particularly bright that late fall day. At about 3:30 that afternoon, I was

9   called to the scene of an accident in which a pedestrian had been struck by a vehicle. I was only a

10   few blocks away, on the corner of Greenview and Whitehead Road, and got there within about

11   two minutes. The accident occurred on Mattis Avenue, just south of Kirby. Mattis is a four-lane

12   road at that point with two lanes in either direction. There is a three-foot concrete median

13   separating the north and southbound lanes. Exhibit 14 is a photo of that median from where it

14   starts at the intersection looking southwest. Exhibit 15 shows the same median looking back up

15   toward Kirby.

[handwritten: Katherine Potter → Ped]

16   *[handwritten: Charles T. Shrackler – driver]*

17   When I arrived at the scene, I found the victim, who I later identified as Katherine Potter, age

18   forty-five, lying underneath a pickup truck. I later identified the driver of the truck as Charles T.

19   Shrackle, age thirty-eight. I asked Mr. Shrackle to move the truck back so that I could have more

20   of an opportunity to provide assistance to Mrs. Potter. He did so. Mrs. Potter was alive and

21   appeared to be conscious. She was moaning and there was a grimace on her face. She appeared to

22   be in a lot of pain. Her eyes were closed for the most part, but she opened them several times.

23   She didn't seem to focus on me or anything else. At one point, it sounded like she said the name

24   "Jeff." She said it maybe three or four times in a row. She didn't say anything else. There was no

25   indication of use of alcoholic beverages either by Mrs. Potter or by Mr. Shrackle.

26

27   The photograph, Exhibit 4, is a fair and accurate depiction of Mrs. Potter as she lay on the

28   pavement before the ambulance arrived after the truck was backed away.

29   *[handwritten: Jim & Ed not on police report]*

30   I waited with Mrs. Potter until the ambulance arrived. After the ambulance took her away, I

31   began in earnest to conduct an investigation. I talked with some other witnesses at the scene,

32   including Jim Marshall and Ed Putnam, who work at the tire store. I also talked to Mr. Shrackle.

33   He told me that he had turned left onto Mattis from Kirby. He said that he felt an impact after he

34   passed the curb south of Kirby Avenue. He remembered that the impact was several seconds after

35   he passed the curb. He didn't know what had happened, but that he took his foot from the

36   accelerator and put it on the brake as hard as he could. He was able to stop the truck and got out

37   and found Mrs. Potter lying underneath it.

38

1   I took measurements of the location of the truck after Mrs. Potter was taken away by the

2   ambulance. The measurements are indicated on my police report. I had Mr. Shrackle move the

3   truck back to the place that it had been, or at least as close as we could figure it was. I measured

4   the distance as fifty-two feet, four inches from the beginning of the crosswalk for pedestrians

5   crossing Mattis on the south side of Kirby. The crosswalk is approximately five feet wide and the

6   limit line on the east side of Mattis is another three feet down from the crosswalk. There were

7   almost seventeen feet of skid marks up to the place where the truck was stopped. These

8   measurements are all on my police accident report, Exhibit 1, which I made as part of my official

9   duties. Based upon the formula that we use, the skid marks would tell us that the truck's

10   minimum speed at the time of the impact would have been 33 miles per hour.

11

12   No, I haven't taken the accident reconstruction courses offered by the department yet, but I

13   got the 33 miles an hour based on this formula they gave us to help estimate speed. No, I don't

14   know whether the formula changes with the type of vehicle. It's just a general formula, I think.

15

16   Based on my investigation, I concluded that no citations were justified. Based on that

17   investigation and my experience, I concluded that Mrs. Potter was out of the crosswalk when she

18   was hit. She was probably fifteen to twenty feet south of the crosswalk at the point of impact.

19

20   The photographs labeled Exhibits 9–21 were taken by me as part of my continuing

21   investigation and at the request of the district attorney's office. They accurately show various

22   views of the intersection of Kirby and Mattis Avenues and environs as they existed on the date of

23   this tragic accident.

24

25   Exhibit 2 is a scale diagram of the intersection of Kirby and Mattis that I obtained from the

26   Nita City Department of Public Works.

27

28   Exhibit 3 is an electronic blow-up of that same intersection showing the various crosswalks

29   and medians. It is to scale. On Exhibits 3a and 3b I placed numbered arrows showing where I

30   was standing as I took the photos marked as Exhibits 9–21 and pointing in the direction I was

31   facing as I took each photo.

32

33

1   I have read the foregoing and it is a true and accurate transcription of my deposition

2 testimony given on October 18, 2002.

3

4

5 *Michael Young*   Date   October 18, 2002

6 Michael Young

7

8 Subscribed and sworn before me this 18th day of October, 2002.

9

10

11 *Harry Gibbons*

12 Harry Gibbons

13 Notary

14

15

16

17

18

19

20

21

22

23

24

25

26

27

28

29

30

31

32

33

34

35

36

37

38

39

40

SUMMARY OF DEPOSITION OF JAMES MARSHALL

1   I am the owner and operator of Jim Marshall's Tires, 1601 Kirby, Nita City, Nita. I have

2   owned and operated the business for fifteen years. We sell Firestone tires and do state inspections

3   and some kinds of car repair including brakes. We also have a self-wash facility.

4

5   I know Charles Shrackle. He has bought tires from us for both his own car and the vehicles

6   used in the construction business. We have also done some inspections and brake work for him.

7   We haven't done any work for them since the accident. Before that time, I'd say he had

8   purchased tires from us a couple of times a year for several years. We had probably inspected all

9   of his cars and trucks.

10

11   I was standing doing some maintenance work on one of the vacuum units for the car wash at

12   about 3:30 on November 30, 2001. It was the second unit from the corner of Mattis. You can see

13   it in the photo marked Exhibit 12, just past the yellow awning. That's my Firestone sign in the

14   background. I saw a dark-haired woman walking east on the south sidewalk of Kirby right in

15   front of my shop.

Page 17

5.   Q. What time was this?

6.   A. About 3:30 in the afternoon.

7.   Q. What did you see?

8.   A. When I first saw the dark-haired woman, she was maybe thirty feet from the

9.   intersection on the sidewalk.

10.   Q. What did she look like?

11.   A. I remember that she seemed to be in her forties or fifties, but I don't remember what

12.   she was wearing or much else about her.

13.   Q. Then what happened?

14.   A. About a minute or minute and a half later I heard a thump coming from the direction

15.   of Mattis Avenue. I ran out to the front of the car wash area and looked toward the spot

16.   where I had heard the thud. It was just south of the intersection on Mattis.

17.   Q. Can you be more specific as to where that spot was?

18.   A. I can't say for sure if the noise came from the area of the crosswalk or was south of

19.   it, but it was real close to that point. No more than five feet south of the crosswalk.

20.   Q: Just to make sure, how long was it from the time you first saw the woman walking

21.   on the sidewalk until you heard the thud?

22.   A: No more than a minute, maybe a minute and a half. I had been talking to a customer

23.   during that time.

1   Exhibit 13 shows my place across the street and the crosswalk Mrs. Potter headed down

2 towards where the person taking this picture was standing. The beginning of the crosswalk is

3 shown on the left.

4

5   When I looked in the direction of Mattis, I saw Mr. Shrackle's Toyota pickup carrying a body

6 in front of it. I realized within a few moments that the truck was one we had inspected belonging

7 to the Shrackle Construction Company. You can't miss a Shrackle Construction vehicle with that

8 logo he has on all the doors. I sent one of my employees to see if he could help and called the

9 police on my cell phone. I then went to help and saw that the injured woman was the same woman

10 I had seen walking east on Kirby.

11

12   I stayed near her until the police arrived. I told the police the same thing I just told you. I also

13 told things to some guy from the insurance company who came to see me a couple of weeks after

14 the accident.

15

16   Exhibit 9 shows the sidewalk outside my business looking east across Mattis towards the

17 White Castle. Mrs. Potter was in the shadow at the bottom of this picture when I first saw her.

18   Exhibit 22 is a statement this investigator fellow wrote up after talking to me a couple weeks

19 after the accident. That's my signature at the bottom and initials at the top. He got a couple of

20 things about me wrong. I think he asked me about those things specifically, so I changed them

21 although I didn't really read the statement very carefully. The investigator was in a hurry to get

22 someplace, so I looked it over real quick and signed it.

23

1   I have read the foregoing and it is a true and accurate transcription of my deposition testimony
2   given on November 27, 2002.
3
4
5   _James Marshall_
6   James Marshall
7
8
9   Subscribed and sworn before me this 27th day of November, 2002.
10
11
12   Harry Gibbons
13   _____
14   Harry Gibbons
15   Notary
16
17
18
19
20
21

SUMMARY OF DEPOSITION OF CHARLES T. SHRACKLE

1   I am Charles T. Shrackle, one of the defendants in this case. I live at 1701 West Johnston, Nita
2 City. I am thirty-eight years old.
3
4   I am a self-employed excavating contractor. I started my business, the Shrackle Construction
5 Company, four years ago. Before that time, I worked for various construction firms as a
6 supervisor. Shrackle is a small business corporation. My wife Emily and I are the only
7 stockholders. Our work usually involves digging trenches for dry wells, sewer or water pipes, or
8 for electrical conduits, and installing the pipes or other hardware necessary for the jobs. We then
9 anchor the job, usually with cement, and after the work is checked and approved, refill the
10 excavation. The firm only does excavation work. We do work for developers, for public utilities,
11 and for state and local government. We have twelve full-time employees, and hire a number of
12 laborers each day depending on what work we are doing. We may have as many as fifteen extra
13 people working for us on any given day. Although much of our equipment is rented to fit our
14 needs for particular jobs, we own some, including a backhoe and a couple of dump trucks. We
15 have an excavator and bulldozer on one-year leases. On November 30, 2001, we were involved in
16 a couple of sewer excavation projects. One was a relatively small one for the city at the corner of
17 John and Holiday Park at the north end of town. The other was a very large project for an
18 extension of the Greenbriar Manor subdivision. Greenbriar Manor is on the south end of town.
19 This project has been giving us some problems. We were past the due date for completion of our
20 portion of the job. It wasn't our fault. We ran into some rock we hadn't expected to find but the
21 general contractor, Clark Poe, was not particularly sympathetic. In fact, Poe had summoned me to
22 a meeting on the afternoon of the accident. As a matter of fact, he had e-mailed me a letter,
23 Exhibit 23, asking me to meet with him, which was a little unusual. We were supposed to meet at
24 the site at about 3:30. Exhibit 24 is the letter I sent back to him by e-mail.
25
26   On the morning of the accident, I got up at 6:45 A.M., my usual time. I had gotten a good
27 night's sleep, probably about seven hours. I was taking no medication and the state of my health
28 was good. I had not had any alcoholic beverages either on the day of the accident or on the day
29 before. I don't use drugs of any kind.
30
31   I started the day at my office, which is in Sommers Township, just at the northeast part of town.
32 I got my crews working by using my cell phone and then went to the John and Holiday Park site. I
33 stayed there most of the day. We were putting the finishing touches on a sewer we had installed. I
34 stayed there until about 2:30 P.M. I then had to make a stop at Nita Builders Supply, which is located
35 near downtown—a couple of miles from the Holiday Park site. I ordered some material there and
36 talked to some of the people in the office. One of the other contractors was talking about how bad
37 business was and how much trouble he was having with some of his subcontractors. He wanted
38 advice on how to cut their charges and how to get them to get their

1   work done on schedule. I was running a little late for my meeting with Poe at Greenbriar, so I cut

2   the conversation short and headed for Greenbriar. I was by myself.

3

4   Greenbriar is located on South Mattis Street, about five miles from where the accident

5   occurred. I would guess I left Builders Supply about ten after three.

Page 22

11.   Q.   What did you do once you left Builders Supply?

12.   A.   I drove down First Street heading out of town. When I got to Kirby I turned right.

13.   Q.   How long did that take?

14.   A.   It's about a half mile to Kirby, so I'd say no more than five or ten minutes.

15.   Q.   Once you turned onto Kirby, what did you do?

16.   A.   I went straight to Mattis so I could turn and head out to Greenbriar. Mattis is about ten

17.   blocks down the way.

18.   Q.   Did you use your cell phone during this time at all?

19.   A.   Yes. As I turned onto Kirby I called Poe on my cell phone to tell him I would be a little

20.   late.

21.   Q.   Tell me about that conversation.

22.   A.   We talked a couple of minutes. Poe told me not to sweat being a little late, but he did say

23.   he had an appointment at 4:00 that he would have to leave for so I should get there as

24.   soon as I could.

25.   Q.   Were you still on the phone when you arrived at Mattis?

26.   A.   I'm not sure. I may have still been talking to him when I got there.

1   When I got to the intersection of Mattis and Kirby, the light was green in my favor. There was
2   moderate traffic. I did not come to a complete stop, but slowed for a car that went by before I
3   could make a left turn to go south on Mattis. I started my turn from the southernmost, westbound
4   lane of Kirby. Exhibit 16 shows the left turn lane I was in on the right side of the photograph, and
5   the median I drove around on Mattis on the left side of the photo. Exhibit 11 shows cars making
6   the same turn I made from Kirby onto Mattis.
7
8   I made a gradual turn to the east southbound lane of Mattis. I observed some schoolchildren,
9   three I think, on the southwest corner of the intersection—where Jim Marshall's car wash is.
10   They were just standing there. I had my eye on them in case one should dart into the path of the
11   car. I didn't know any of the kids and I don't remember much else about them. I think I also
12   observed a crossing guard on the southeast corner of the street. I don't remember any other
13   pedestrians.
14
15   I remember making the turn and there was the impact and that was it. The impact took place
16   several seconds after I passed south of the Kirby Avenue sidewalk. I was probably about four feet
17   west of the median.
18
19   I did not see Mrs. Potter before the impact. I did not apply my brakes before the impact,
20   although as I made the turn I had my foot on the brake pedal. I usually make my left turns that
21   way. I was probably traveling about fifteen miles an hour at the time of the impact.
22
23   I remember that it was a clear day and that the sun was out. It bothered me a little as I was
24   making the turn because Mattis at that point goes southwest and at that time of day the sun was
25   pretty low in the sky. I could still see in front of me. I had my eye on the children on the corner
26   all the time.
27
28   I both heard and felt the impact, but I didn't immediately know what I had hit. The impact was
29   on the left front of my vehicle. As soon as I felt the impact, I applied the brakes with as much
30   force as I could. As I said, my foot was already on the brake. The vehicle stopped quickly and I
31   jumped out. I moved around the front of the car and I saw Mrs. Potter lying under it. She was
32   lying almost straight, with her head under the front bumper and her feet straight back. Her head
33   was pointed south and her feet north. She seemed to be conscious, and I asked her, "Where did
34   you come from?" She didn't reply.
35
36   The police arrived almost immediately. We got a first aid kit out of my truck and applied a
37   compress to her forehead and we waited for the ambulance to come. There were skid marks and
38   the police measured them. There was a mark on the lefthand side of the hood of my truck, near
39   the division between the hood and the fender.
40
41

1   At the time of the accident I was driving a 2001 Toyota Tacoma truck. My truck was in good
2   condition at the time of the accident. I had had the car inspected and the brakes checked about a
3   month before the accident. As a matter of fact, Jim Marshall did the inspection. The tires were
4   relatively new. I think they had less than 5,000 miles on them. Exhibit 6 shows me and my truck
5   at a job site out in Ferndale just after I got it. That's the kind of cell phone I use, the hand-held
6   kind. The logo shown on the truck in that exhibit and more closely in Exhibit 7 is my company
7   logo.

8

9   At the time of the accident, I was covered by an automobile liability policy of $500,000 per
10   person and $1 million per accident. The policy was with Boston Casualty. The policy number is
11   FA606560, effective September 23, 2001 to September 23, 2002. Except for the fact that there is
12   concern that this action will exceed the policy limits, the insurance company hasn't indicated any
13   problem with my coverage. I also have a $5 million umbrella policy for the company with Boston
14   Casualty. They have also been notified about this accident.

15

16   I did not meet with Clark Poe at Greenbriar that day. Shortly after they took Mrs. Potter away in
17   the ambulance, I called him on my cell phone and told him what had happened. We met the next
18   day. Based on our conversation, there was a reduction in the amount we were to be paid for the job.
19   I wasn't too happy about the result, but compared to Mrs. Potter's situation it was no big deal.

20

21   Ordinarily it would take me about twenty minutes to get from Builders Supply to Greenbrier.
22   However, it could take longer on weekday afternoons about that time because of the schools
23   getting out. The traffic was a little heavy before I got to the intersection of Kirby and Mattis, but
24   not too bad. I thought that it might get worse after I turned on Mattis, particularly down about a
25   mile when the road narrows. It's highway at that point, but two lanes. But I felt I'd make it in
26   plenty of time for my meeting with Poe.

27

28   I have read the foregoing and it is a true and accurate transcription of my deposition testimony
29   given on December 17, 2002.

30

31

32   Signed ___*Charles T. Shrackle*___   Date ___December 17, 2002___
33   _____Charles T. Shrackle

34

35   Subscribed and sworn before me this 17th day of December, 2002.

36

37

38   *Terry Anderson*_____

39   Terry Anderson
40   Notary

41

SUMMARY OF DEPOSITION OF JEFFREY POTTER

1   I am Jeffrey Potter, the plaintiff in this case, and I live in the same house that Katherine and I

2   lived in before her death, at 4920 Thorndale in Nita City. I am forty-nine years of age. I'm a

3   professor in the physics department at the University of Nita. I received a bachelor's degree in

4   physics from Purdue and a doctorate in physics from the University of Wisconsin/Madison. I

5   received my Ph.D. twenty-four years ago and have been at the University of Nita since 1983.

6

7   Katherine and I were married twelve years ago, June 15, 1990. We met because we sang in

8   the same community chorus. She was a high school computer science teacher then. She got a

9   B.S. in computer science from Nita City University in 1977. She worked on her Ph.D. in

10   computer science from 1977 to 1979, but never finished. She had done all of her course work,

11   but had not completed her dissertation. She told me she decided that she could accomplish more

12   for herself and the world by teaching in high school and she didn't need a Ph.D. to do that. But,

13   by the time we met in 1988, she was disillusioned with teaching. She was tired of working as

14   hard as you do as a high school teacher and not making much money.

15

16   Shortly after we got married she left teaching and began working for Techno-Soft, Inc., a

17   software company. She loved the work at Techno-Soft and was making a great deal more money.

18   She became very ambitious in her work situation, but not so much that we didn't have a good time

19   together. I was busy with my work as well, so our schedule and career goals were compatible.

20

21   Despite both of our involvement in our work, Katherine and I had other interests and spent a

22   great deal of time together. We would go to movies and out to dinner whenever we could. We

23   also liked to sing and we stayed with the community chorus. She had a beautiful alto voice; I am

24   a so-so bass. We would almost always make the practices, which were once a week. There were

25   concerts about four times a year and we would rehearse even more frequently as we got closer to

26   concert time.

27

28   We also loved to travel, particularly to Europe. I had the summers free and we would take

29   every three-week vacation that Katherine had to travel. Tuscany and Umbria were our favorites.

30   We loved to walk in the Italian countryside or have a glass of wine or coffee at a sidewalk café.

31   We had a pretty special relationship until Shrackle took her life. I think we had about as near

32   perfect a relationship as is possible in a marriage.

33

34   I did write the letter to Dr. Stevens marked Exhibit 28. As I said in the letter, I thought our

35   marriage would work out just fine. Kathy and I, like most couples had some difficulties over the

36   years. She was always driven by her work, both teaching and with Techno-Soft, and that was an

37   ongoing problem. We also disagreed ultimately about having children. We tried to achieve a

38   pregnancy early on in our marriage and had difficulties. After a lot of testing, the doctors couldn't

39   identify a problem, but we still never conceived. I wanted to explore in vitro fertilization and/or

1   adoption, but Kathy was ultimately opposed and we resigned ourselves to our very comfortable life.
2   Around the time of Kathy's death, we were having a disagreement over retirement. I wanted Kathy
3   to take an early retirement so we could travel more, and she wanted to continue working. She was
4   very ambitious. We were working through that problem with Dr. Stevens at the time that Kathy
5   was killed. Although it was a bone of contention it did not threaten our marriage. Although I said in
6   the letter that I might seek another relationship if our marriage didn't work out, that was a remote
7   possibility. We had always been able to work out our problems, whatever they were. No, I did not
8   have another relationship in mind at that time or at any time during our marriage, and I resent your
9   insinuation. I was completely faithful to Kathy and she to me. After Kathy died, I saw Dr. Stevens
10 briefly, maybe three times, and he helped me with my grieving, but ultimately you have to learn to
11 live with your loss and time is the best healer.
12
13   Katherine had done well at Techno-Soft and they seemed to like her. Although times are
14 tough in the software business, Techno-Soft has done fairly well.

Page 18

14. Q. How did Katherine like her work?

15. A. Techno-soft gave her very interesting work projects, although she had to work

16. long hours, and she certainly enjoyed making some real money after all those

17. years in teaching.

18. Q. How did you feel about her work?

19. A. I liked the fact she found her work rewarding, but I thought she might want to take

20. it easy and spend more time traveling.

21. Q. Had you talked to her about the possibility of retiring?

22. A. I had talked to her now and again about retiring and traveling with me during the

23. summers. She seemed to be interested in the idea, but hadn't agreed to it. I

24. suggested to her that those years might be better spent enjoying herself traveling.

1   We had a "50-50 equal partnership" marriage. All of our income was pooled and we shared

2   household chores equally. We shared all of the things that have to be done to maintain a home

3   and a relationship. I did most of the cooking and shopping for food. Kathy did most of the

4   laundry and cleaning. We liked to do gardening together and split those chores. I did most of the

5   repair work around the house like minor electrical or plumbing problems, but Kathy was the

6   better painter and when the house needed inside painting, Kathy did that. Kathy was in charge of

7   the finances. She did the bills each month, wrote out checks on the computer. She also did the

8   banking and the taxes. Although we talked about the investments we made, Kathy was really

9   more interested and knew more about the stock market. I followed her advice in allocating my

10   University retirement account among different mutual funds. She was very good at that. I was the

11   one who planned our travel. I liked to do that and had more time than Kathy in light of

12   everything else she did and her job, which was demanding.

13

14   I will never forget hearing about Katherine's accident—if you can call that kind of

15   recklessness on Shrackle's part an accident. I was in my office talking to one of my students,

16   Cheryl Tobias, when the departmental secretary knocked on the door and told me that Katherine

17   had been in a serious accident. I rushed over to the hospital, Nita Memorial, and found her in the

18   emergency room. She was unconscious when I first saw her. Later, in the intensive care unit, her

19   eyes would open from time to time but she never said anything. She would generally moan softly

20   during both her waking moments and even when she seemed to be unconscious. She appeared to

21   be in considerable pain the whole time in the hospital.

22

23   I stayed at the hospital during the days before her death. Friends brought me clean clothes and

24   I was able to shower there. Those were the longest four days of my life. Even when the doctors

25   were pessimistic, I was hopeful for a miracle, but it just didn't happen. When she died, I just

26   went back to the empty house. It took me six months before I could begin to clear out some of

27   her clothes, books, and papers. I still haven't cleared it all out. I can't believe what has happened

28   to me since Kathy's death. I sit at home day after day, watching television or listening to music. I

29   can't even read a book. I seldom go out, except to teach my classes. I am sure that my teaching

30   has suffered. Certainly, I no longer have the close working relationship with my students that I

31   had when Kathy was alive. I'm alone all the time and I'm lonely.

32

33   Our house is located two blocks down from Greenview Avenue on the east side of the street.

34   I assume Kathy was walking home at the time she was struck down by Mr. Shrackle. Kathy and I

35   loved to walk through Senn Park. There were times we would walk through the park rather than

36   walking all the way down Thorndale from Kirby just to enjoy the beauty of the park.

37

38   Exhibit 5 is a fair and accurate depiction of Katherine as she looked before the accident. The

39   photograph was taken in our backyard about a year before her death.

40

41   Yes, as I mentioned, I do know a young woman named Cheryl Tobias. She was and is a

graduate student at the University and she had just completed a class with me as a teaching
assistant in the fall semester of 2001 when Kathy died. I believe I said that she was actually in my
office when I got the news about Kathy's injuries. Yes, she and I have a developed a personal
relationship since Kathy's death. I have not supervised any of her work since the Fall, 2001
semester. That would be inconsistent with having a personal relationship. Despite our age
difference, she's twenty-four, we have a lot in common and Cheryl shares my interest in
traveling. Yes, Exhibits 29 and 30 are travel records from a trip we took together to Martinique
and Exhibit 30 is a copy of our bill from that same trip. Exhibit 32 is a photo of Cheryl and me.
Our relationship is developing slowly. We have been intimate but Cheryl has not moved in with
me or me with her and we have no plans to do so. I can't say what will happen in the future. Our
age difference doesn't bother Cheryl, but I'm concerned it will become a problem in the future.
Also, she has her whole career ahead of her. She's very bright and I don't know how that will
jibe with my work plans in the future. Although I value my relationship with Cheryl and she's
helped me deal with Kathy's death, she'll never take Kathy's place in my heart and I doubt my
relationship with Cheryl will ever be as fulfilling as what I had with Kathy. We were soul mates
and I think that only happens once in your life if you're lucky.

Yes, I still live in the same house Kathy and I bought together.

Exhibit 26 is the bill from Nita Memorial Hospital, which has been paid. Exhibit 27 is the
invoice from the funeral home, which also has been paid.

I have read the foregoing and it is a true and accurate transcription of my deposition
testimony given November 28, 2002.

Signed ___*Jeffrey T. Potter*___   Date ___November 28, 2002___
_____ Jeffrey Potter
Subscribed and sworn before me this 28th day of November, 2002.

___*Harry Gibbons*___
Harry Gibbons,
Notary

SUMMARY OF DEPOSITION OF DANIEL SLOAN

1   I am forty-eight years old. I am the principal shareholder and chief executive officer of

2   Techno-Soft, Inc. We are a small company with about fifty employees. We provide software for

3   various high-tech manufacturing companies. The software we have developed is used in delicate

4   manufacturing processes in the electronics industry.

5

6   Katherine Potter started working for us in 1990. Her starting salary was $34,000 a year. Her

7   salary increased on an annual basis until, in 2001, she was making a base salary of $85,000 in the

8   position of Technology Training Specialist. At the time of her death, her fringe benefits package

9   was 20 percent of her salary. This included contribution to the retirement plan, medical and

10   dental insurance, as well as life and disability insurance. As an example of what we thought of

11   her, we gave her a bonus of $2,000 in January, 2001. The bonus was in part simply a recognition

12   of her value to the company but it was also in recognition of the fact that she had spent more than

13   ten years with us. Through our human resources director, Linda Graham, I provided all of the

14   details of her employment to Robert Glenn, the economist working for Mr. Potter's lawyer.

15

16   Katherine was one of our prize employees. She had consistently received raises at the highest

17   level of all employees. I fully expected her to continue that pattern. She was smart and worked

18   very hard. She also was very ambitious. She kept talking about all those years she spent working

19   for peanuts as a high school teacher. In fact, I was grooming her to become an executive vice-

20   president, she was that good. No, it wasn't certain that she would be made a vice-president. If she

21   did receive that promotion and there was a better than even chance, in my opinion, that she

22   would have, it likely would have occurred in three or so years, by about 2005 or 2006. The

23   current salary range for that position is $120,000–$150,000 a year. Also, people at that level

24   typically receive bonuses in the $10,000 range based on good performance. Our business is

25   expanding and Katherine was exactly the kind of person we needed. She had all of the technical

26   skills as well as an extraordinary ability to work with people.

27

28   Katherine did tell me that her husband, Jeffrey, was always after her to retire early. He's a

29   college professor and has the summers off. They both loved to travel. Katherine told me that this

30   was a dream of Jeff's and she had told him that she would think about it. She told me that there

31   was no way that she would retire before she was sixty. She told me that she loved her job and

32   that all of the things she did with Jeff were okay, but work was really her first love. I am

33   absolutely confident she would have stayed on.

34

35   Even in the very remote possibility that she would have left her current duties, she could have

36   gone on a part-time basis. A number of our employees in their fifties have done that and, given

37   the nature of our work, we can accommodate them by permitting them to work at home.

38

39

1   We'll sure miss Katherine. I hope that Jeffrey gets through all of this in one piece. I've
2   always seen him as pretty fragile guy.
3
4
5   I have read the foregoing and it is a true and accurate transcription of my deposition
6   testimony given November 29, 2002.
7
8
9   Signed _____   Date ____November 29, 2002____
10   Daniel Sloan
11
12
13   Subscribed and sworn before me this 29th day of November, 2002.
14
15   _Harry Gibbons_
16   _____
17   Harry Gibbons
18   Notary
19
20
21
22
23
24
25
26
27
28
29
30
31
32
33
34
35
36
37
38
39

State of Nita Circuit Court
Circuit Court of Darrow County
Civil Division

Jeffrey T. Potter, the Administrator of the Estate of Katherine Potter,
and Jeffrey T. Potter, individually
(Plaintiff)
v.
Charles T. Shrackle and The Shrackle Construction Company
(Defendants)

dated: July 1, 2002

Introduction

I, Robert Glenn, understand this matter involves Jeffrey T. Potter, the Administrator of the Estate of Katherine Potter, and Jeffrey T. Potter, individually, as plaintiff, and Charles T. Shrackle and The Shrackle Construction Company (collectively, "Shrackle") as defendants. As I understand this matter, Ms. Katherine Potter was struck by an automobile driven by Mr. Charles T. Shrackle on November 30, 2001. Ms. Potter died on December 4, 2001 as a result of injuries sustained in that accident.

Engagement of Robert Glenn

As part of this engagement, Madden & James, counsel for plaintiffs, requested that I:
1. Review the Potter v. Shrackle case file, including but not limited to:
    a. the complaint and answer;
    b. statements of Marilyn J. Kelly, Juanita Williams, Victoria Williams, Alice Mallory, Benjamin Grimson;
    c. depositions of James Marshall, Victoria Williams, Michael Young, Charles T. Shrackle, Jeffrey Potter, and Daniel Sloan; and
    d. other documents provided by counsel;
2. Collect information relevant to a calculation of economic losses resulting from a wrongful death; and
3. Provide economic and statistical analysis regarding plaintiff's specific claims.

In preparing my analysis, I have relied on counsel, Madden & James, for any interpretation of legal issues.

Supplemental Analysis and Opinions

I understand that discovery in this matter is still ongoing and that additional documents, statements, deposition or trial testimony on topics relevant to the opinions issued in this report may be forthcoming. As a result, I reserve the right to supplement this report or to address any such testimony at trial.

Opinion

Based upon my continuing review and analysis of the Potter v. Shrackle case file, supplemented with my own research of relevant economic and demographic information, I have developed the following opinion regarding economic damages in this matter.
1. From the date of her death through her eventual retirement at age 60, the value of Katherine Potter's lost earnings, benefits and household work, net of her consumption is a loss of $2,334,579 to her estate and to her husband, Jeffrey Potter. In present discounted value, this amount is a loss of $1,532,021 to the plaintiff.

Bases for Opinions

1. Katherine Potter was in good health at the time of her death and would have reasonably been expected to work until at least the age of 60 before her retirement.

2. Katherine Potter was happy with her position as a Technology Training Specialist at Techno-Soft, Inc. I believe the pattern of her salary growth from the date of her death to her eventual retirement at age 60 would be similar to the average pattern of salary growth during her period of employment with the company.

3. Katherine Potter would have continued to enjoy her fringe benefits as an employee of Techno-Soft, Inc. I have spoken with Ms. Linda Graham, Human Resources Director at Techno-Soft, Inc. and have learned that Katherine Potter's benefits amounted to 20% of her income at the time of her death.

4. Katherine Potter shared equally in the household work with her husband, Jeffrey Potter, and her death will result in a loss equal to the value of Katherine's labor, which equaled approximately $41 per hour at the date of her death.

Exhibits

For purposes of presenting our opinions and their bases, I may develop and use exhibits including overheads, flip charts, and other summary graphics. I may also use certain demonstrative aids and illustrations in presenting technical concepts and analyses.

Compensation

The hourly rates for myself and my research associates who worked on this matter range between $75 and $350 per hour. My hourly rate is $350 per hour.

Qualifications

I am a Professor of Economics at the University of Nita in Nita City with fields of concentration in labor economics and microeconomics. I hold a bachelors degree in economics from the University of North Carolina (1985) and a Ph.D. in economics from the University of Illinois (1989). I have taught economics at the undergraduate and graduate level at the University of Nita for fourteen years as well as numerous seminars in industry. As part of my duties as a professor at a research institution, I direct graduate research, conduct independent research, and publish my results in academic economic journals. In addition to my publications, I have received research grants from the National Science Foundation, the Social Science Research Council, the Center for Comparative Studies at the University of Nita, and the Nita Law Enforcement Commission.

July 1, 2002

Robert Glenn
Professor of Economics, University of Nita

POTTER v. SHRACKLE AND THE SHRACKLE CONSTRUCTION COMPANY
DAMAGES MODEL OF ROBERT GLENN, PH.D.
TABLE 1. SUMMARY OF ECONOMIC LOSS, WRONGFUL DEATH OF KATHERINE POTTER

SUMMARY OF ECONOMIC LOSS

		Nominal Dollars	*Present Discounted Value*
A.	Future Value of Earnings	$2,918,363	$1,915,118
B.	Future Value of Fringe Benefits	$583,673	$383,024
C.	Future Value of Household Work	$1,024,233	$672,133
D.	Future Value of Personal Consumption	$2,191,691	$1,438,254
E.	Total Value of Loss (A + B + C - D)	$2,334,579	$1,532,021

POTTER v. SHRACKLE AND THE SHRACKLE CONSTRUCTION COMPANY
DAMAGES MODEL OF ROBERT GLENN, PH.D.
TABLE 2. FUTURE VALUE OF EARNINGS OF KATHERINE POTTER, AGE 45 TO 60

Date of Birth:	June 15, 1956
Date of Death:	December 4, 2001
Appraisal Period	2002 to 2016
Projected Retirement Age:	60
Discount Rate:	6.00%
Earnings Growth Rate:	9.80%

Year	Projected Age	*Projected Value of Earnings*	*Present Discounted Value of Earnings*
2001	45	$85,000	
2002	46	$93,329	$93,329
2003	47	$102,474	$102,474
2004	48	$112,515	$106,146
2005	49	$123,540	$109,950
2006	50	$135,645	$113,890
2007	51	$148,936	$117,971
2008	52	$163,530	$122,199
2009	53	$179,554	$126,578
2010	54	$197,147	$131,114
2011	55	$216,465	$135,813
2012	56	$237,676	$140,680
2013	57	$260,965	$145,721
2014	58	$286,536	$150,943
2015	59	$314,612	$156,353
2016	60	$345,440	$161,956
Value of Future Earnings:		**$2,918,363**	**$1,915,118**

Potter v. Shrackle Case File

POTTER v. SHRACKLE AND THE SHRACKLE CONSTRUCTION COMPANY
DAMAGES MODEL OF ROBERT GLENN, PH.D.
TABLE 3. HISTORICAL EARNINGS GROWTH OF KATHERINE POTTER, 1978 TO 2001

Date of Birth:	June 15, 1956	
Date of Death:	December 4, 2001	
Observation Period:	1978 to 2001	

Year	Age	Earnings	% Change from Previous Year	Job
1978 to 1980	22-24	$0	n/a	(1)
1981	25	$19,000	n/a	(2)
1982	26	$19,600	3.2%	(2)
1983	27	$20,250	3.3%	(2)
1984	28	$20,900	3.2%	(2)
1985	29	$21,600	3.3%	(2)
1986	30	$22,300	3.2%	(2)
1987	31	$23,000	3.1%	(2)
1988	32	$23,750	3.3%	(2)
1989	33	$24,500	3.2%	(2)
1990	34	$25,400	3.7%	(2)/(3)
1991	35	$34,000	33.9%	(3)
1992	36	$42,000	23.5%	(3)
1993	37	$50,000	19.0%	(3)
1994	38	$57,500	15.0%	(3)
1995	39	$62,500	8.7%	(3)
1996	40	$67,500	8.0%	(3)
1997	41	$71,000	5.2%	(3)
1998	42	$73,500	3.5%	(3)
1999	43	$76,000	3.4%	(3)
2000	44	$78,000	2.6%	(3)
2001	45	$85,000	9.0%	(3)
2002	Deceased	$0	-100.0%	Deceased

Average Income Growth Rate (1992 to 2001): | 9.80% |

Job Information:

(1) Attending Graduate School, University of Nita
(2) Computer Instructor, Nita City Unified School District
(3) Computer Instructor, Techno-Soft, Inc.

POTTER v. SHRACKLE AND THE SHRACKLE CONSTRUCTION COMPANY
DAMAGES MODEL OF ROBERT GLENN, PH.D.
TABLE 4. FUTURE VALUE OF FRINGE BENEFITS OF KATHERINE POTTER, AGE 45 TO 60

Date of Birth:	June 15, 1956
Date of Death:	December 4, 2001
Appraisal Period	2002 to 2016
Projected Retirement Age:	60
Discount Rate:	6.00%
Benefits as % of Income	20.00%

Year	Projected Age	Projected Value of Fringe Benefits	Present Discounted Value of Fringe Benefits
2001	45	$17,000	
2002	46	$18,666	$18,666
2003	47	$20,495	$20,495
2004	48	$22,503	$21,229
2005	49	$24,708	$21,990
2006	50	$27,129	$22,778
2007	51	$29,787	$23,594
2008	52	$32,706	$24,440
2009	53	$35,911	$25,316
2010	54	$39,429	$26,223
2011	55	$43,293	$27,163
2012	56	$47,535	$28,136
2013	57	$52,193	$29,144
2014	58	$57,307	$30,189
2015	59	$62,922	$31,271
2016	60	$69,088	$32,391
Value of Future Fringe Benefits:		**$583,673**	**$383,024**

Potter v. Shrackle Case File

Date of Birth:	June 15, 1956
Date of Death:	December 4, 2001
Appraisal Period	2002 to 2016
Projected Retirement Age:	60
Discount Rate:	**6.00%**
# of Hours Per Day at Household Work	**2**
Days Per Year Doing Household Work	**365**

Year	Projected Age	Projected Value of Household Work	Present Discounted Value of Household Work
2001	45	$29,832	
2002	46	$32,755	$32,755
2003	47	$35,964	$35,964
2004	48	$39,488	$37,253
2005	49	$43,358	$38,588
2006	50	$47,606	$39,971
2007	51	$52,271	$41,403
2008	52	$57,393	$42,887
2009	53	$63,016	$44,424
2010	54	$69,191	$46,016
2011	55	$75,971	$47,665
2012	56	$83,415	$49,373
2013	57	$91,589	$51,143
2014	58	$100,563	$52,975
2015	59	$110,417	$54,874
2016	60	$121,236	$56,840
Value of Future Household Work:		**$1,024,233**	**$672,133**

Assumption:

(1)   There are 2,080 work hours in a year (52 weeks * 40 hours per week).

POTTER v. SHRACKLE AND THE SHRACKLE CONSTRUCTION COMPANY
DAMAGES MODEL OF ROBERT GLENN, PH.D.
TABLE 6. FUTURE VALUE OF PERSONAL COMPSUMPTION OF KATHERINE POTTER, AGE 45 TO 60

Date of Birth:	June 15, 1956
Date of Death:	December 4, 2001
Appraisal Period:	2002 to 2016
Projected Retirement Age:	60
Discount Rate:	**6.00%**
Consumption as % of Income	**75.10%**

Year	Projected Age	Projected Value of Personal Consumption	Present Discounted Value of Personal Consumption
2001	45	$63,835	
2002	46	$70,090	$70,090
2003	47	$76,958	$76,958
2004	48	$84,499	$79,716
2005	49	$92,778	$82,572
2006	50	$101,869	$85,531
2007	51	$111,851	$88,597
2008	52	$122,811	$91,772
2009	53	$134,845	$95,060
2010	54	$148,058	$98,467
2011	55	$162,565	$101,996
2012	56	$178,495	$105,651
2013	57	$195,985	$109,437
2014	58	$215,188	$113,359
2015	59	$236,274	$117,421
2016	60	$259,425	$121,629
Value of Future Consumption:		**$2,191,691**	**$1,438,254**

TABLE 6 NOTES

(1)   To arrive at Katherine Potter's net contribution to Potter household welfare (i.e. what Jeffrey Potter will lose monetarily as a result of his wife's death), the future value of Katherine's consumption expenditures should be subtracted from the future value of her income, fringe benefits, and household work.

(2)   The U.S. Department of Labor has calculated that, on average, household expenditures amount to 89.1% of household income for American households.

(3)   Of this amount, on average, 28% of household income is spent on housing expenses.

(4)   In this matter, half of this amount should be excluded from Katherine Potter's share of income spent on household expenses since housing is a benefit equally shared by both Katherine and Jeffrey Potter. Katherine's death is a loss to Mr. Potter insofar as Katherine contributed to the cost of housing for their household.

(5)   As a result, 75.1% of Katherine's future wage and salary earnings should be subtracted from her total wage and salary earnings to account for the value of her expenditures.

Source

U.S. Department of Labor, Bureau of Labor Statistics, Consumer Expenditures in 1999, May 2001, Report 949, Table 2.

CURRICULUM VITAE
Robert Glenn, Ph.D.
Arthur Anderson Professor of Economics
University of Nita, Department of Economics, Campus Locator #43
Nita City, Nita
(020) 444-2308, Fax (020) 444-2307
glennecon@email.nita.edu

Education

B.S. University of North Carolina (1984) (economics)

Ph.D. University of Illinois (1988) (economics)

Employment History

Assistant Professor, University of Nita, 1988-84

Associate Professor, University of Nita 1994-98

Professor, University of Nita, 1999-2002

Arthur Anderson Professor, 2002-

Principal publications since 1992:

Books

Microeconomics in a Time of Terrorism, Oxford University Press (2002)

Loss Evaluation in Wrongful Death Cases, Aspen (2000)

Articles

"The Effect of September 11 on Microeconomic Theory," 80 Harvard Public Policy Review 1769 (2002)

"Is Your Loss Worth Anything?" 5 Journal of Law and Economics 1289 (2000)

"Can Our Economic System Survive a Terrorist Attack?" 45 Economics and Politics 549 (1999)

"Valuing Services and Potential Retirement," 19 Journal of Labor Economics 42 (1995)

Sample expert testimony

(I have been qualified as an expert in economics in 24 different cases. I have testified for the plaintiff in all but 3 cases.)

Michaels v. Hammer, North Carolina Superior Court, October 2002 (personal injury, testified for plaintiff)

Smith v. Tucker, United States District Court (SDNY) (personal injury, testified for plaintiff)

Rosen v. Nichol, United States District Court (S. D. Calif.) (wrongful death, testified for plaintiff)

Glandon v. Schwartz, Nita Superior Court, May, 1999 (wrongful death case, testified for plaintiff)

State of Nita Circuit Court
Circuit Court of Darrow County
Civil Division

Jeffrey T. Potter, the Administrator of the Estate of Katherine Potter,
and Jeffrey T. Potter, individually
(Plaintiff)
v.
Charles T. Shrackle and
The Shrackle Construction Company
(Defendants)

Expert Report of Elizabeth Buchanan, Ph.D.
Assistant Professor of Economics, Nita State University
Nita City, Nita

September 1, 2002

1.0 Introduction

I, Elizabeth C. Buchanan, Ph.D., understand this matter involves Jeffrey T. Potter, the Administrator of the Estate of Katherine Potter, and Jeffrey T. Potter, individually, as plaintiff, and Charles T. Shrackle and The Shrackle Construction Company (collectively, "Shrackle") as defendants. As I understand this matter, Ms. Katherine Potter was struck by an automobile driven by Mr. Charles T. Shrackle on November 30, 2001. Ms. Potter died on December 4, 2001 as a result of injuries sustained in that accident.

2.0 Qualifications

I am an Assistant Professor of Economics at Nita State University with fields of concentration in labor economics and industrial organization. I am also a graduate of the University of Nita, holding both a bachelors and doctorate degree in economics. I have taught at Nita State University for the past five years: two years as a visiting professor, two years as a lecturer and one year as an assistant professor. Appendix A is a copy of my current resume. It contains a listing of my papers and publications for the past 10 years.

2.1 Engagement of Elizabeth Buchanan

As part of this engagement, James Barber of Pierce, Johnson & Clark ("Pierce"), counsel for defendants Shrackle, requested that I:
- Review the expert report on damages prepared by Dr. Robert Glenn;

- Review the Potter v. Shrackle case file, including but not limited to:
  - the complaint and answer;
  - depositions of James Marshall, Victoria Williams, Michael Young, Charles T. Shrackle, Jeffrey Potter, and Daniel Sloan;
  - statements of Marilyn J. Kelly, Juanita Williams, Victoria Williams, Alice Mallory, Benjamin Grimson; and
  - other documents which I have reviewed which have been produced in this matter;

- Collect information relevant to a calculation of economic losses resulting from a wrongful death; and

- Provide economic and statistical analysis regarding plaintiff's specific claims.

In preparing my analysis, I have relied on counsel, Pierce, for any interpretation of legal issues.

2.2 Supplemental Analysis and Opinions

I understand that discovery in this matter is still ongoing and that additional documents, statements, deposition or trial testimony on topics relevant to the opinions issued in this report may be forthcoming. As a result, I reserve the right to supplement this report or to address any such testimony at trial.

3.0 Opinion

Based upon my continuing review and analysis of Dr. Glenn's expert report and the Potter v. Shrackle case file, supplemented with my own research of relevant economic and demographic information, I have developed the following opinion regarding economic damages in this matter.

- Dr. Robert Glenn substantially overstates the total value of loss allegedly suffered by the plaintiff due to incorrect and inappropriate assumptions used in his damages model.

- In my own opinion, from the date of her death through her eventual retirement at age 55, the value of Katherine Potter's lost earnings, benefits and household work, net of her consumption is a loss of $411,077 to her estate and to her husband, Jeffrey Potter. In present discounted value, this amount is a loss of $333,719 to the plaintiff.

4.0   Bases for Opinions

- It is my opinion that Katherine Potter would have reasonably been expected to work full-time until the age of 50 and then would work part-time until her retirement at age 55. Deposition testimony from her husband, Jeffrey Potter, stated that he and Katherine talked about taking an early retirement. My calculations of loss valuation is conservative in that it treats Katherine as having worked to the age of 55, which would tend to overstate the loss if she were to retire before that age.

- It is my opinion that Katherine Potter would have an average annual salary increase of five percent per year. Dr. Glenn averages Katherine's salary increases during her entire period of employment at Techno-Soft, Inc. This method would overstate the salary increases Katherine would likely receive in the period after her death. I note that her salary increases are smaller and smaller, in percentage terms, and thus the use of a long-run averages would be ignorant of this trend. Instead, I use an average of her annual salary increases over the last three years to capture the fact that she may be reaching the upper salary limit of her position.

- I assume that the imputed value of benefits enjoyed by Katherine Potter is 17.5% of her annual salary. Like Dr. Glenn, I have spoken to Linda Graham, Human Resources Director at Techno-Soft, Inc. Based upon my discussion with Ms. Graham, I learned that Dr. Glenn's calculation of future fringe benefits overstates this value since it ignores the fact that Katherine Potter received a special one-time bonus payout of $2,000 in 2001 for staying beyond ten years at Techno-Soft, Inc. Were this one-time payout to be removed, the actual rate of benefits would be lowered from 20% to 17.5% of her annual salary. Dr. Glenn thus overstates all future projections for fringe benefit calculations since he does not appropriately evaluate the baseline year. I use the more justifiable number of 17.5% in my projections.

- Although Katherine Potter shared equally in the household work with her husband, Jeffrey Potter, and her death will result in a loss equal to the value of Katherine's labor, I disagree with Dr. Glenn's methodology of using her imputed hourly wage as the appropriate replacement wage. Katherine's hourly wage, assuming a 2,080-hour work year, is imputed to be approximately $41 per hour. Dr. Glenn uses this amount as the value of Katherine's lost labor. This methodology is incorrect in that Dr. Glenn should value the loss of Katherine's household labor at its replacement cost. Since many of the household tasks did not require the use of Katherine's specialized skills, I use a more appropriate measure of replacement cost, the minimum wage.

- It is my opinion that, as a member of the Potter household, Katherine Potter consumed approximately 75% of her annual income as her personal consumption. The amount of consumption that Mrs. Potter consumed for her benefit out of her income should not be included in an award of damages to Mr. Potter as he did not necessarily benefit from this consumption during Mrs. Potter's lifetime. Although Mrs. Potter would continue to consume as a member of the household after her retirement, in order to be conservative in the estimate of damages, I exclude this amount from the calculation of loss to Mr. Potter. Inclusion of this stream of consumption of retirement would make the damages amount even smaller as Mrs. Potter would continue to consume but not be earning any wage or salary income.

In sum, these inappropriate and inaccurate assumptions used by Dr. Glenn in his model result in a significant overstatement of any likely damages suffered. I believe that he may have overstated damages by as much as a factor of four. I believe that damages suffered by the plaintiff would not have exceeded $334,000.

5.0 Exhibits

For purposes of presenting our opinions and their bases, I may develop and use exhibits including overheads, flip charts, and other summary graphics. I may also use certain demonstrative aids and illustrations in presenting technical concepts and analyses.

6.0 Compensation

The hourly rates for myself and my research associates who worked on this matter range between $50 and $250 per hour. My hourly rate is $250 per hour.

Elizabeth C. Buchanan
Assistant Professor of Economics
Nita State University
Nita City, Nita

September 1, 2002

POTTER v. SHRACKLE AND THE SHRACKLE CONSTRUCTION COMPANY
REBUTTAL DAMAGES MODEL OF ELIZABETH C. BUCHANAN, PH.D.
TABLE 1. SUMMARY OF ECONOMIC LOSS, WRONGFUL DEATH OF KATHERINE POTTER

SUMMARY OF ECONOMIC LOSS

		Nominal Dollars	*Present Discounted Value*
A.	**Future Value of Earnings**	$807,964	$680,250
B.	**Future Value of Fringe Benefits**	$141,394	$119,044
C.	**Future Value of Household Work**	$68,500	$45,293
D.	**Future Value of Personal Consumption**	$606,781	$510,868
E.	**Total Value of Loss (A + B + C - D)**	$411,077	$333,719

POTTER v. SHRACKLE AND THE SHRACKLE CONSTRUCTION COMPANY
REBUTTAL DAMAGES MODEL OF ELIZABETH C. BUCHANAN, PH.D.
TABLE 2. FUTURE VALUE OF EARNINGS OF KATHERINE POTTER, AGE 45 TO 60

Date of Birth:	June 15, 1956	
Date of Death:	December 4, 2001	
Appraisal Period	2002 to 2016	
Projected Retirement Age:	55	
Discount Rate:	**6.00%**	
Earnings Growth Rate:	**5.00%**	

Year	Projected Age	% of Full-Time Employment	Projected Value of Earnings	Present Discounted Value of Earnings
2001	45	100%	$85,000	
2002	46	100%	$89,252	$89,252
2003	47	100%	$93,717	$93,717
2004	48	100%	$98,405	$92,835
2005	49	100%	$103,328	$91,961
2006	50	100%	$108,497	$91,096
2007	51	50%	$56,962	$45,119
2008	52	50%	$59,811	$44,695
2009	53	50%	$62,803	$44,274
2010	54	50%	$65,945	$43,857
2011	55	50%	$69,244	$43,445
2012	56	0%	(RETIRED)	(RETIRED)
2013	57	0%	(RETIRED)	(RETIRED)
2014	58	0%	(RETIRED)	(RETIRED)
2015	59	0%	(RETIRED)	(RETIRED)
2016	60	0%	(RETIRED)	(RETIRED)
Value of Future Earnings:			**$807,964**	**$680,250**

POTTER v. SHRACKLE AND THE SHRACKLE CONSTRUCTION COMPANY
REBUTTAL DAMAGES MODEL OF ELIZABETH C. BUCHANAN, PH.D.
TABLE 3. HISTORICAL EARNINGS GROWTH OF KATHERINE POTTER, 1978 TO 2001

Date of Birth:	June 15, 1956	
Date of Death:	December 4, 2001	
Observation Period:	1978 TO 2001	

Year	Age	Earnings	% Change from Previous Year	Job
1978 to 1980	22-24	$0	n/a	(1)
1981	25	$19,000	n/a	(2)
1982	26	$19,600	3.2%	(2)
1983	27	$20,250	3.3%	(2)
1984	28	$20,900	3.2%	(2)
1985	29	$21,600	3.3%	(2)
1986	30	$22,300	3.2%	(2)
1987	31	$23,000	3.1%	(2)
1988	32	$23,750	3.3%	(2)
1989	33	$24,500	3.2%	(2)
1990	34	$25,400	3.7%	(2)/(3)
1991	35	$34,000	33.9%	(3)
1992	36	$42,000	23.5%	(3)
1993	37	$50,000	19.0%	(3)
1994	38	$57,500	15.0%	(3)
1995	39	$62,500	8.7%	(3)
1996	40	$67,500	8.0%	(3)
1997	41	$71,000	5.2%	(3)
1998	42	$73,500	3.5%	(3)
1999	43	$76,000	3.4%	(3)
2000	44	$78,000	2.6%	(3)
2001	45	$85,000	9.0%	(3)
2002	Deceased	$0	-100.0%	Deceased

Average Income Growth Rate (1999 to 2001): | 5.00% |

Job Information:

(1) Attending Graduate School, University of Nita

(2) Computer Instructor, Nita City Unified School District

(3) Computer Instructor, Techno-Soft, Inc.

POTTER v. SHRACKLE AND THE SHRACKLE CONSTRUCTION COMPANY
REBUTTAL DAMAGES MODEL OF ELIZABETH C. BUCHANAN, PH.D.
TABLE 4. FUTURE VALUE OF FRINGE BENEFITS OF KATHERINE POTTER, AGE 45 TO 60

Date of Birth:	June 15, 1956
Date of Death:	December 4, 2001
Appraisal Period	2002 to 2016
Projected Retirement Age:	55
Discount Rate:	6.00%
Benefits as % of Income	17.50%

Year	Projected Age	Projected Value of Fringe Benefits	Present Discounted Value of Fringe Benefits
2001	45	$14,875	
2002	46	$15,619	$15,619
2003	47	$16,400	$16,400
2004	48	$17,221	$16,246
2005	49	$18,082	$16,093
2006	50	$18,987	$15,942
2007	51	$9,968	$7,896
2008	52	$10,467	$7,822
2009	53	$10,991	$7,748
2010	54	$11,540	$7,675
2011	55	$12,118	$7,603
2012	56	(RETIRED)	(RETIRED)
2013	57	(RETIRED)	(RETIRED)
2014	58	(RETIRED)	(RETIRED)
2015	59	(RETIRED)	(RETIRED)
2016	60	(RETIRED)	(RETIRED)
Value of Future Fringe Benefits:		**$141,394**	**$119,044**

POTTER v. SHRACKLE AND THE SHRACKLE CONSTRUCTION COMPANY
REBUTTAL DAMAGES MODEL OF ELIZABETH C. BUCHANAN, PH.D.
TABLE 5. FUTURE VALUE OF HOUSEHOLD WORK OF KATHERINE POTTER, AGE 45 TO 60

Date of Birth:	June 15, 1956
Date of Death:	December 4, 2001
Appraisal Period	2002 to 2016
Projected Retirement Age:	55
Discount Rate:	6.00%

	Before Retirement	During Retirement
# of Hours Per Day at Household Work	2	4
Days Per Year Doing Household Work	250	250
Total Hours Per Year	500	1000

Year	Projected Age	Hourly Replacement Wage for Household Work	Projected Value of Household Work	Present Discounted Value of Household Work	
2001	45	$6.00	$3,000		
2002	46	$6.00	$3,000	$3,000	
2003	47	$6.00	$3,000	$3,000	
2004	48	$6.00	$3,000	$2,830	
2005	49	$6.00	$3,000	$2,670	
2006	50	$6.50	$3,250	$2,729	
2007	51	$6.50	$3,250	$2,574	
2008	52	$6.50	$3,250	$2,429	
2009	53	$6.50	$3,250	$2,291	
2010	54	$7.00	$3,500	$2,328	
2011	55	$7.00	$3,500	$2,196	
2012	56	$7.00	$7,000	$4,143	(RETIRED)
2013	57	$7.00	$7,000	$3,909	(RETIRED)
2014	58	$7.50	$7,500	$3,951	(RETIRED)
2015	59	$7.50	$7,500	$3,727	(RETIRED)
2016	60	$7.50	$7,500	$3,516	(RETIRED)

Value of Future Household Work: **$68,500**   **$45,293**

POTTER v. SHRACKLE AND THE SHRACKLE CONSTRUCTION COMPANY
REBUTTAL DAMAGES MODEL OF ELIZABETH C. BUCHANAN, PH.D.
TABLE 6. FUTURE VALUE OF PERSONAL CONSUMPTION OF KATHERINE POTTER, AGE 45 TO 60

Date of Birth:	June 15, 1956
Date of Death:	December 4, 2001
Appraisal Period:	2002 to 2016
Projected Retirement Age:	55
Discount Rate:	6.00%
Consumption as % of Full-Time Income	75.10%

Year	Projected Age	Projected Value of Personal Consumption	Present Discounted Value of Personal Consumption
2001	45	$63,835	
2002	46	$67,028	$67,028
2003	47	$70,381	$70,381
2004	48	$73,902	$69,719
2005	49	$77,599	$69,063
2006	50	$81,481	$68,413
2007	51	$42,778	$33,885
2008	52	$44,918	$33,566
2009	53	$47,165	$33,250
2010	54	$49,525	$32,937
2011	55	$52,002	$32,627
2012	56	(RETIRED)	(RETIRED)
2013	57	(RETIRED)	(RETIRED)
2014	58	(RETIRED)	(RETIRED)
2015	59	(RETIRED)	(RETIRED)
2016	60	(RETIRED)	(RETIRED)
Value of Future Consumption:		**$606,781**	**$510,868**

CURRICULUM VITAE
Dr. Elizabeth C. Buchanan

Business Address: Department of Economics, DB # 234
Nita State University, CB# 233
Nita City, Nita
(020) 555-4387
Fax: (020) 555-4388
E-mail: ebuchan@email.nsu.edu

Education: B.S., University of Nita, 1988 (economics)
Ph.D. University of Nita, 1992 (economics)

Current position: Assistant Professor of Economics, Nita State University. Concentration in labor economics and industrial organization.

Employment history: Assistant Professor of Economics, Nita State University since 1997.

Dunhill Consultants, private economics consulting group, 1992-1997

Principal publications since 1992:

"The Value of Household Services," 18 Journal of Labor Economics 284 (1994)

"Damage Assessment for the Infringement of Intellectual Property Rights," 82 Contemporary Economics Problems 1204 (1998)

"Economic Loss in Copyright Cases," 4 Journal of Law and Economics 48 (1999)

"Can We Accurately Evaluate Lost Wages?" 7 Journal of Law and Economics 87 (2001)

"Intellectual Property and Modern Economic Thought," 80 Harvard Public Policy Review 438 (2002)

Expert Testimony: Homer v. Underhill, Nita Superior Court, June 1997 (personal injury case, testified for the plaintiff with regard to economic loss resulting from injury)

Glandon v. Schwartz, Nita Superior Court, May, 1999 (wrongful death case, testified for defendant with regard to economic loss resulting from death)

Marydale v. Farrer, Nita Superior Court, September, 2001 (personal injury case, testified for the defendant with regard to economic loss resulting from injury)

MEMORANDUM

To: Robert Glenn, Ph.D.

From: Steve Dyer, Research Assistant

Date: September 16, 2002

Re: *Potter v. Shrackle*

CONFIDENTIAL

Per your request, I've read through Dr. Buchanan's expert report in the Potter case. Contrasting her analysis with yours, I think the following points are important.

First, Dr. Buchanan assumes that Katherine Potter will completely stop working at age 55. In his deposition, Daniel Sloan, her boss, stated that "She told me that there was no way that she would retire before she was sixty." Dr. Buchanan doesn't address this testimony in her expert report. In fact, the deposition testimony of Jeffrey Potter indicates that, although he mentioned early retirement to her, Katherine did not agree to it.

Second, Dr. Buchanan does not include the possibility that Mrs. Potter might be promoted, which would result in an increase in Mrs. Potter's annual salary. Mr. Sloan mentioned in his deposition that his "business is expanding" and "Mrs. Potter was exactly the kind of person" the business needed because "she had all of the technical skills as well as an extraordinary ability to work with people." Mr. Sloan even goes as far as saying that he "was grooming her to become an executive vice-president." This indicates that it is very likely that Mrs. Potter would have been promoted before she retired and would have received a commensurate boost in her salary. Dr. Buchanan assumes that she won't be promoted and her salary growth is stagnant.

Third, Dr. Buchanan understates the value of Mrs. Potter's fringe benefits as a percentage of her annual salary. She uses 17.5% percent of Mrs. Potter's salary to calculate benefits. However, the actual amount of benefits, excluding the $2,000 bonus, is closer to 17.65%. Even though it is probably not a large difference in terms of damages, it is an inaccuracy in her report. More importantly, I believe your estimates using 20% for the fringe benefits package is correct. In his deposition, Daniel Sloan states, "At the time of her death, her fringe benefits package was 20% of her salary. This included contribution to a retirement plan, medical and dental insurance, as well as life and disability insurance." Based upon this statement, the $2,000 bonus is not included in the 20% which Mr. Sloan talks about. I think Dr. Buchanan was confused when she talked to Linda Graham and thought the $2,000 was included in Mr. Sloan's 20% figure for fringe benefits.

Fourth, Dr. Buchanan uses the minimum wage as the replacement cost for the loss of Mrs. Potter's household labor. Some household chores, however, should be valued at more than the minimum wage, such as cooking and gardening, as Mr. Potter really could not find somebody to do such things for minimum wage. In addition, to the extent that Mrs. Potter had specialized skills (such as managing the household finances, preparing tax returns, etc.), the value of her lost work should be valued at its replacement cost, which would likely be higher than the minimum wage.

On the other hand, I note in your report that you use Mrs. Potter's imputed hourly wage at Techno-Soft, Inc. to value her lost household work. I think the calculation comes out to be somewhere around $41 per hour for her imputed wage. Even if Dr. Buchanan underestimates the value of Mrs. Potter's lost household work using the hourly minimum wage, I think using her imputed Techno-Soft, Inc. wage may overstate the value of her lost household work insofar as it would not take someone making $41 per hour to do basic, unskilled household work.

Fifth, both you and Dr. Buchanan use the same discount rate in your calculations.

Sixth, both you and Dr. Buchanan use the same consumption rate in your calculations.

I will continue to look for more documents that can better support our arguments. In the meantime, I will come by your office later in the week so that you can approve my time sheet.

JURY INSTRUCTIONS

Preliminary Instructions

1 - Introduction

You have been selected as jurors and have taken an oath to well and truly try this cause. This trial will last one day.

During the progress of the trial there will be periods of time when the Court recesses. During those periods of time, you must not talk about this case among yourselves or with anyone else. Do not talk to any of the parties, their lawyers or any of the witnesses.

You should keep an open mind. You should not form or express an opinion during the trial and should reach no conclusion in this case until you have heard all of the evidence, the arguments of counsel, and the final instructions as to the law that will be given to you by the Court.

2 - Conduct of the Trial

First, the attorneys will have an opportunity to make opening statements. These statements are not evidence and should be considered only as a preview of what the attorneys expect the evidence will be.

Following the opening statements, witnesses will be called to testify. They will be placed under oath and questioned by the attorneys. Documents and other tangible exhibits may also be received as evidence. If an exhibit is given to you to examine, you should examine it carefully, individually, and without any comment.

It is counsel's right and duty to object when testimony or other evidence is being offered that he or she believes is not admissible.

When the Court sustains an objection to a question, the jurors must disregard the question and the answer, if one has been given, and draw no inference from the question or answer or speculate as to what the witness would have said if permitted to answer. Jurors must also disregard evidence stricken from the record.

When the Court sustains an objection to any evidence the jurors must disregard that evidence. When the Court overrules an objection to any evidence, the jurors must not give that evidence any more weight than if the objection had not been made.

When the evidence is completed, the attorneys will make final statements. These final statements are not evidence but are given to assist you in evaluating the evidence. The attorneys are also permitted to argue in an attempt to persuade you to a particular verdict. You may accept or reject those arguments as you see fit.

Finally, just before you retire to consider your verdict, I will give you further instructions on the law that applies to this case.

Potter v. Shrackle Case File

FINAL INSTRUCTIONS

1.   Members of the jury, the evidence and arguments in this case have been completed, and I will now instruct you as to the law.

The law applicable to this case is stated in these instructions and it is your duty to follow all of them. You must not single out certain instructions and disregard others.

It is your duty to determine the facts, and to determine them only from the evidence in this case. You are to apply the law to the facts and in this way decide the case. You must not be governed or influenced by sympathy or prejudice for or against any party in this case. Your verdict must be based on evidence and not upon speculation, guess, or conjecture.

From time to time the court has ruled on the admissibility of evidence. You must not concern yourselves with the reasons for these rulings. You should disregard questions and exhibits that were withdrawn or to which objections were sustained.

You should also disregard testimony and exhibits that the court has refused or stricken.

The evidence that you should consider consists only of the witnesses' testimonies and the exhibits the court has received.

Any evidence that was received for a limited purpose should not be considered by you for any other purpose.

You should consider all the evidence in the light of your own observations and experiences in life.

Neither by these instructions nor by any ruling or remark that I have made do I mean to indicate any opinion as to the facts or as to what your verdict should be.

2.   You are the sole judges of the credibility of the witnesses and of the weight to be given to the testimony of each witness. In determining what credit is to be given any witness, you may take into account his or her ability and opportunity to observe; his or her manner and appearance while testifying; any interest, bias, or prejudice he or she may have; the reasonableness of the testimony considered in the light of all the evidence; and any other factors that bear on the believability and weight of the witness' testimony.

3.   You have heard evidence in this case from witnesses who testified as experts. The law allows experts to express an opinion on subjects involving their special knowledge, training and skill, experience, or research. While their opinions are allowed to be given, it is entirely within the province of the jury to determine what weight shall be given their testimony. Jurors are not bound by the testimony of experts; their testimony is to be weighed as that of any other witness.

4. The law recognizes two kinds of evidence: direct and circumstantial. Direct evidence proves a fact directly; that is, the evidence by itself, if true, establishes the fact. Circumstantial evidence is the proof of facts or circumstances that give rise to a reasonable inference of other facts; that is, circumstantial evidence proves a fact indirectly in that it follows from other facts or circumstances according to common experience and observations in life. An eyewitness is a common example of direct evidence, while human footprints are circumstantial evidence that a person was present.

The law makes no distinction between direct and circumstantial evidence as to the degree or amount of proof required, and each should be considered according to whatever weight or value it may have. All of the evidence should be considered and evaluated by you in arriving at your verdict.

5. When I say that a party has the burden of proof on any issue, or use the expression "if you find," "if you decide," or "by a preponderance of the evidence," I mean that you must be persuaded from a consideration of all the evidence in the case that the issue in question is more probably true than not true.

Any findings of fact you make must be based on probabilities, not possibilities. It may not be based on surmise, speculation, or conjecture.

6. One of the parties in this case is a corporation, and it is entitled to the same fair treatment as an individual would be entitled to under like circumstances, and you should decide the case with the same impartiality you would use in deciding a case between individuals.

7. The Court will now instruct you on the claims and defenses of each party and the law governing the case. You must arrive at your verdict by unanimous vote, applying the law, as you are now instructed, to the facts as you find them to be.

8. Plaintiff claims that Charles Shrackle was negligent in his operation and control of the pickup truck and that his negligence caused Katherine Potter's injuries and death. Plaintiff seeks damages for defendants' negligence both on behalf of himself individually and as the administrator of Katherine Potter's estate. Thus, plaintiff has brought this lawsuit and is claiming damages in two separate capacities: (1) as an individual for the injury and loss suffered by him as Katherine Potter's husband, and
(2) as the administrator of Katherine Potter's estate for the pain, suffering, and expenses incurred by her prior to her death.

Defendants deny that Charles Shrackle was negligent or that his negligence caused Katherine Potter's injuries and death. Defendants claim that Katherine Potter was negligent, and that it was her own negligence that caused her injuries and death.

9. In this case, the plaintiff, Jeffrey Potter, has the burden of proving:

(1)   That Charles Shrackle was negligent, and

(2)   That the negligence of Charles Shrackle proximately caused Katherine Potter's death.

The defendants have the burden of proving:

(1)   That the deceased, Katherine Potter, was negligent, and

(2)   That the negligence of Katherine Potter was a proximate cause of her death.

Thus, each of the parties to this case has a burden of proof to maintain, and you are to determine whether they have met their burdens. Your task is to determine whether Charles Shrackle or Katherine Potter, or both, were negligent, and the extent to which their negligence caused Katherine Potter's injuries and death.

10. The terms "negligent" or "negligence" as used in these instructions mean the failure to use that degree of care that an ordinarily careful and prudent person would use under the same or similar circumstances.

11. The terms "contributorily negligent" or "contributory negligence" mean negligence on the part of the deceased Katherine Potter.

12. It is the duty of every person using a public street or highway, whether a pedestrian or a driver of a vehicle, to exercise ordinary care to avoid placing himself, herself, or others in danger and to exercise ordinary care to avoid a collision.

13. The violation of a statute, if you find any, is negligence as a matter of law. Such negligence has the same effect as any other act or acts of negligence.

A statute in the state of Nita provides:

(1)   That the driver of a motor vehicle shall yield the right of way, by slowing down or stopping if necessary, to a pedestrian crossing the roadway within a crosswalk when the pedestrian is upon that half of the roadway in which the vehicle is traveling, or when either the vehicle or the pedestrian is approaching that half of the roadway so closely that the pedestrian is in danger.

(2)   That a pedestrian crossing a roadway at any point other than within a marked crosswalk shall yield the right of way to all vehicles upon the roadway.

(3)   This right of way, however, is not absolute but rather creates a duty to exercise ordinary care to avoid collisions upon the party having the right of way.

14. Proximate cause is that cause which, in a natural and continuous sequence, produces the injury, and without which the injury would not have occurred.

To be a proximate cause of Katherine Potter's injuries and death, negligent conduct by either Charles Shrackle or Katherine Potter need not be the only cause, nor the last or nearest cause. It is sufficient if the negligent conduct acting concurrently with another cause produced the injury.

Thus, there need not be only one proximate cause of Katherine Potter's injuries and death, and you may find that the negligence of both Charles Shrackle and Katherine Potter was the proximate cause of her death. On the other hand, you may find that the negligence of either of them was the sole proximate cause of her death.

15. You are to determine the negligence, if any, of both Charles Shrackle and Katherine Potter, and then to apportion the responsibility of each.

Please state your findings of negligence in the following form:

We find the conduct of the defendant, Charles Shrackle, was _____% negligent.

We find that the conduct of the deceased, Katherine Potter, was _____% negligent.

16. In this case you must also decide the issue of damages. You must determine the amount which will reasonably and fairly compensate Jeffrey Potter for the losses resulting from the death of his wife, Katherine Potter.

In determining the loss to the plaintiff, Jeffrey Potter, you should consider the following factors:

(1) Expenses for care, treatment, and hospitalization incident to the injury to Katherine Potter resulting in her death;

(2) Compensation for the pain and suffering of the decedent;

(3) The reasonable funeral expenses of the decedent;

(4) The present monetary value of the decedent to the persons entitled to receive the damages recovered, including but not limited to compensation for the loss of the reasonably expected

   (a) net income of the decedent;
   (b) services, protection, care, and assistance of the decedent, whether voluntary or obligatory, to the persons entitled to the damages recovered;
   (c) society, companionship, comfort, guidance, kindly offices, and advice of the decedent to the persons entitled to the damages recovered;

(5) Nominal damages when the jury so finds.

17.   In determining the amount of damages to the plaintiff, you may consider how long the plaintiff is likely to live, how long the decedent was likely to have lived, that some persons work all their lives and others do not, that a person's earnings may remain the same or may increase or decrease in the future.

In calculating the amount of damages, you must not simply multiply the life expectancies by the annual damages. Instead, you must determine the present cash value for any award of damages. "Present cash value" means the sum of money needed now, which together with what that sum will earn in the future, will equal the amount of the benefits at the times in the future when they would have been received.

18.   The Court did not in any way and does not by these instructions give or intimate any opinions as to what has or has not been proven in the case, or as to what are or are not the facts of the case.

No one of these instructions states all of the law applicable, but all of them must be taken, read, and considered together as they are connected with and related to each other as a whole.

You must not be concerned with the wisdom of any rule of law. Regardless of any opinions you may have as to what the law ought to be, it would be a violation of your sworn duty to base a verdict upon any other view of the law than that given in the instructions of the court.

IN THE CIRCUIT COURT OF
DARROW COUNTY, NITA
CIVIL DIVISION

Jeffrey T. Potter, Administrator of the Estate   )
of Katherine Potter, and   )
Jeffrey T. Potter, individually,   )
)
    Plaintiffs,   )
)
v.   )   **JURY VERDICT**
)   (Interrogatories)
Charles T. Shrackle and the   )
Shrackle Construction Company,   )
)
    Defendants.   )

The jury is to answer the following interrogatories. The foreperson is to answer the interrogatories for the jury and sign the verdict.

Interrogatory No. 1:

Please state your findings of negligence in the following form:

We find that the conduct of the defendant, Charles Shrackle, was _____% negligent.

We find that the conduct of the deceased, Katherine Potter, was _____% negligent.

Interrogatory No. 2:

Please determine the amount of damages to the plaintiff, Jeffrey Potter, both individually and as administrator of Katherine Potter's estate:

Amount _____$

The percentage of negligence that you find to be apportioned to the defendant, Charles Shrackle (Interrogatory No.1) is multiplied by the amount of damages you determine (Interrogatory No. 2), and that amount will be the verdict for the plaintiff, Jeffrey Potter.

The members of the jury have unanimously answered the interrogatories in the manner that I have indicated.

_____
Foreperson

Exhibit 1

Police Report

DEPARTMENT OF TRANSPORTATION BUREAU OF SAFETY PROGRAMMING AND ANALYSIS T & S BUILDING, NITA CITY, NITA	NITA CITY POLICE ACCIDENT REPORT	REPORTABLE ☐ UNREPORTABLE ☐ HAZARDOUS MATERIALS ☐

DATE OF ACCIDENT _11-30-01_ [ ]A.M. [x]P.M. DAY OF WEEK _FRIDAY_ HOUR _3:28_ [ ]A.M. [x]P.M.

TIME POLICE NOTIFIED OF ACCIDENT _11-30-01 3:28_ [ ]A.M. [x]P.M. TIME ARRIVED AT SCENE _3:31_ [ ]A.M. [x]P.M. NUMBER VEHICLES INVOLVED: _1_

OCCURRED IN _DARROW_ COUNTY TOWN OR CITY OF _NITA CITY_

ON STREET: (OR HWY. NO.) _MATTIS_ AT ITS INTERSECTION WITH: (STREET OR HWY. NO.)_____

IF NOT AT INTERSECTION: _52_ [ ]MILES [x]FEET [ ]N [ ]E [ ]S [ ]W FROM _KIRBY_ TOWARD_____
(STREET OR HIGHWAY NUMBER) (STREET OH HIGHWAY NUMBER)

[ ]RT [ ]LFT RUN OFF ROAD [ ]NON-COLLISION ON ROAD [x]PEDESTRIAN [ ]COLLISION OF MOTOR VEHICLE ON ROAD WITH:_____

ROAD DEFECTS:	LIGHT CONDITIONS:	Vehicle 1 VEHICLE TYPE	Vehicle 2	VEHICLE 1 APPARENT CONDITION VEHICLE 2
NONE	DAYLIGHT	2001 TOYOTA Pick-up w/CABOVER /		DRIVER/PEDESTRIAN: NORMAL — DRIVER/PEDESTRIAN: CONDITION UNKNOWN
ROAD CONSTRUCTION:	TRAFFIC CONTROL:	Vehicle 1 LOCALITY	Vehicle 2	PASSENGER: [ ]_____ PASSENGER: [ ]_____
CONCRETE	STOP AND GO SIGNAL	BUSINESS DISTRICT / NO VISION OBSTRUCTION		[ ]_____ [ ]_____
ROAD FEATURE:	WEATHER:	Vehicle 1 VIOLATION INDICATED	Vehicle 2	[ ]_____ [ ]_____
INTERSECTION OF TWO ROADS	CLEAR	NONE		[ ]_____ [ ]_____ APPARENT SOBRIETY: APPARENT SOBRIETY:
ROAD DEFECTS:	ROAD CHARACTER:	Vehicle 1 VEHICLE CONDITION	Vehicle 2	Vehicle 1 HAD NOT BEEN DRINKING Vehicle 2/Pedestrian HAD NOT BEEN DRINKING
NONE	STRAIGHT, LEVEL ROAD	NO DEFECTS DETECTED		INJURIES (INCLUDE FATAL INJURIES)

DESCRIBE WHAT HAPPENED

#1 WAS SOUTHBOUND ON MATTIS AFTER TURNING LEFT FROM KIRBY HE THEN STRUCK PEDESTRIAN APPROX 30'S. OF PEDESTRIAN CROSSWALK. #1 SAID HE DIDN'T SEE PEDESTRIAN UNTIL AFTER HE STRUCK HER. WITNESSES (A) (MOTHER & DAUGHTER) HAD BEEN IN CAR DRIVING EAST ON KIRBY AND SAW PEDESTRIAN RUNNING ACROSS STREET WESTBOUND. NEITHER SAW ACTUAL CONTACT. 12/2/01 WITNESS (B) CALLED STATION AND SAID PEDESTRIAN WAS IN CROSSWALK.

WITNESSES
(A) JUANITA AND VICKY WILLIAMS (B) MRS. MARILYN KELLY
NAME AND ADDRESS 1010 W. KIRBY #15 1910 EDEN LANE
NITA NITA
NAME AND ADDRESS

Michael Young 7219 CITY 11/30/01
OFFICER'S RANK AND NAME (SIGN HERE) NUMBER DEPARTMENT DATE OF REPORT

Veh.	Age	Sex	Race	Inj. Cl.	Name Address
P	28	F	W	A	KATHERINE POTTER 4920 THORNDALE AVE (DIED 12-4-01 5 P.M.)

INJURED TAKEN TO: CITY HOSPITAL

WHAT DRIVERS WERE DOING BEFORE ACCIDENT
VEHICLE ONE:
GOING STRAIGHT AHEAD

VEHICLE TWO:
CROSSING NOT AT INTERSECTION

V E H 1	FIRST CHARLES T.	MIDDLE	LAST SHRACKLE

STREET OR ROAD 1701 W. JOHNSTON CITY AND STATE NITA CITY ZIP ___ AGE 37 DOB 5-13-64 SEX M RACE W
LICENSE NUMBER V311-5114 T16 NITA VEHICLE YR 01 MAKE Toy PU w/CABOVER COLOR GOLDEN-TAN REGISTRATION 237952B NITA 2001 OWNED BY DRIVER
DIRECTION OF TRAVEL [ ]N [ ]E [x]S [ ]W ON MATTIS VEH. REMOVED TO DESTINATION

V E H 2	FIRST KATHERINE	MIDDLE	(PEDESTRIAN) LAST POTTER

STREET OR ROAD 4920 THORNDALE AVENUE CITY AND STATE NITA CITY ZIP ___ AGE 45 DOB 6-15-56 SEX F RACE W
LICENSE NUMBER ___ VEHICLE YR ___ MAKE ___ COLOR ___ REGISTRATION ___ OWNED BY ___
DIRECTION OF TRAVEL [ ]N [ ]E [ ]S [ ]W

Police Report Diagram

Exhibit 1

DEPARTMENT OF TRANSPORTATION BUREAU OF SAFETY PROGRAMMING AND ANALYSIS T & S BUILDING, NITA CITY, NITA	NITA CITY POLICE ACCIDENT REPORT—PAGE 2	REPORTABLE ☐ UNREPORTABLE ☐ HAZARDOUS MATERIALS ☐

Potter v. Shrackle Case File

Exhibit 2

DIAGRAM OF INTERSECTION

Potter v. Shrackle Case File

Potter v. Shrackle Case File

Exhibit 3

ELECTRONIC DIAGRAM OF INTERSECTION

Exhibit 3a

Exhibit 3b

Exhibit 3c

ELECTRONIC DIAGRAM WITH ARROWS

ELECTRONIC DIAGRAM WITH ARROWS

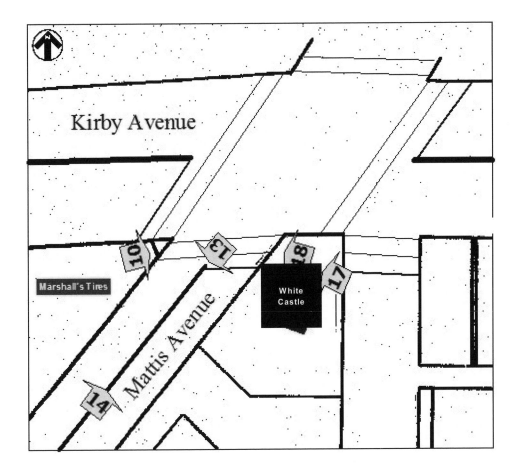

Exhibit 4

PHOTO OF KATHERINE POTTER AT SCENE

Exhibit 5

PHOTO OF KATHERINE POTTER WHILE ALIVE

Exhibit 6

PHOTO OF CHARLES SHRACKLE

Exhibit 7

PHOTO OF SHRACKLE TRUCK

Exhibit 8

PHOTO OF SHRACKLE TRUCK

Exhibit 9

SIDEWALK BORDERING MARSHALL'S

Exhibit 10

ACROSS TO WHITE CASTLE

Exhibit 11

WHERE SHRACKLE TURNED FROM

Exhibit 12

DOWN CROSSWALK TO MARSHALL'S

Exhibit 13

ENTIRE CROSSWALK TOWARD MARSHALL'S

Exhibit 14

LOOKING UP MEDIAN

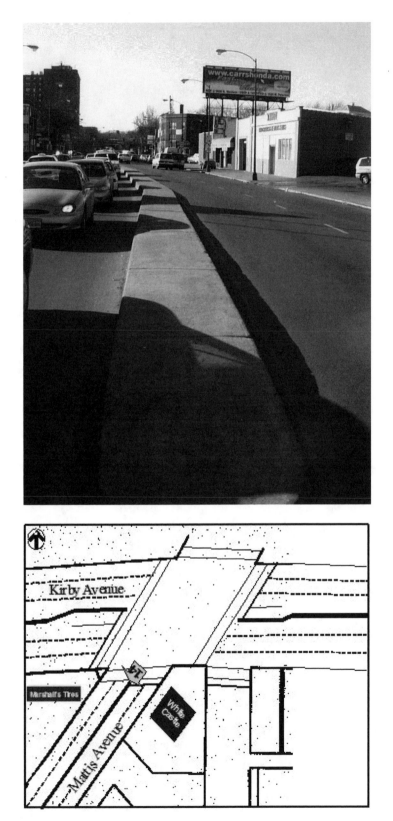

Exhibit 15

LOOKING DOWN MEDIAN

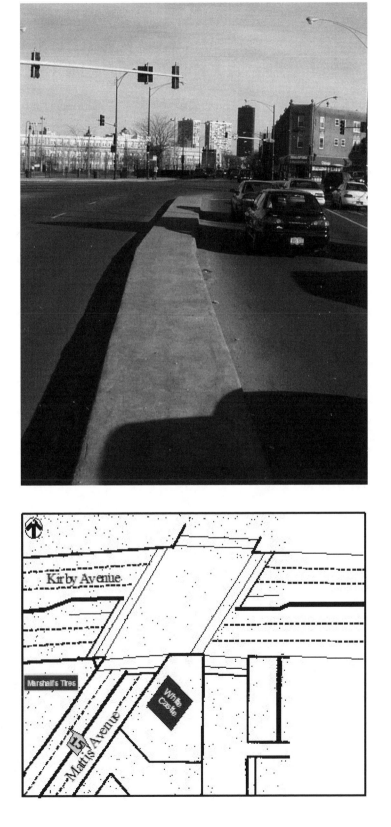

Exhibit 16

MEDIAN NEXT TO SHRACKLE TURN LANE

Exhibit 17

VICTORIA'S VANTAGE

Exhibit 18

VICTORIA'S VANTAGE

Exhibit 19

WHITE CASTLE DRIVE-IN

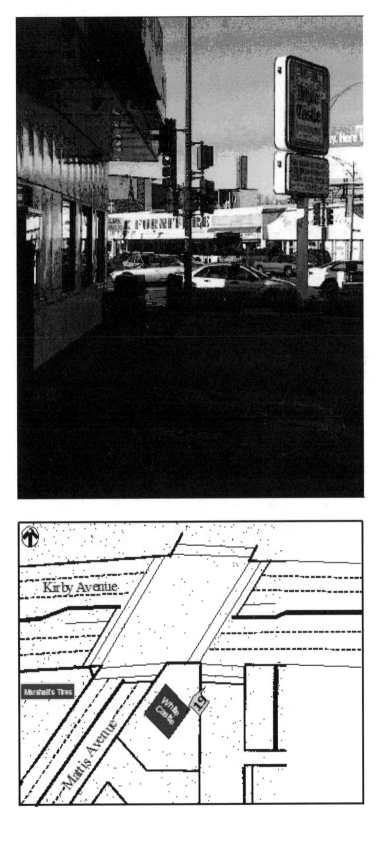

Exhibit 20

WHITE CASTLE TOWARDS MARSHALL'S

Exhibit 21

WHITE CASTLE UP MATTIS

Exhibit 22

STATEMENT OF JAMES MARSHALL

Statement of James Marshall

I am the owner-operator of Jim Marshall's tires, 1601 Kirby, Nita City, Nita. I was working in the car wash portion of my business on Nov. 30, 2001.

At approximately 3:30 on Nov. 30, 2001, I was doing some maintenance work on one of the vacuum units for the car wash. It was the ~~first~~ second from the corner. I saw a dark-haired woman walking east on the south sidewalk of KIRBY. When I saw her, she was 15 or 20 feet from the intersection. I looked over at my employee, Ed Putnam, to ask him something about the job we were doing. About a minute or minute and a half later I heard a thump. I looked out and saw a pickup truck carrying a body on the front of it. I sent Putnam out to see if he could be of help while I called the police. I went out to see if I could be of help and saw the same woman that I'd seen earlier walking east on KIRBY lying on the pavement.

Signed: James Marshall
Witness: Joseph Lucey
Dec. 12, 2001

Editor's Note: **Marshall's business is located on the southwest corner of Kirby and Mattis. This statement was taken by Joseph Lucey, an adjuster for the defendant's insurance carrier, on December 12, 2001, at about 11 A.M. The statement was written by Mr. Lucey. The signature and the correction are in Marshall's handwriting.**

Exhibit 23

Greenbriar - Message - Microsoft Word

File Edit View Insert Format Tools Table Window Help   Type a question for help

Send   Options...   HTML   Sent: Wednesday, 11/28/2001 4:34 PM

To...   Charles Shrackle

Cc...

Subject: Greenbriar

Charlie: The delays on the Greenbriar project are unacceptable. We are so far behind that the developer, Mr. Green, is about ready to cancel the job and get a new contractor. Legally, he can probably do it.

I know that you've had some trouble with rock, but there is always trouble with rock in this area. We need to finish this job immediately.

Come to the job site at 3:30 P.M. on November 30 and be ready to give me a detailed description of your problems and a firm commitment on a conclusion date. This has become a real problem, Charlie, so be there and be on time.

Clark

Clark Poe Construction Company
414 Whitebread Road
Nita City, Nita   99992
(606) 828-1891
cpoe@poecon.com

Greenbriar - Message - Microsoft Word

File   Edit   View   Insert   Format   Tools   Table   Window   Help   Type a question for help

Send   Options...   HTML   Sent: Thursday, 11/29/2001 7:42 AM

To...   cpoe@poecon.com

Cc...

Subject: Greenbriar

Clark: I hear you loud and clear. I'll be there at 3:30 on Friday. Unlike sometimes in the past, I assure you I won't be late.

Charlie

Charles T. Shrackle
Shrackle Construction Company
Route 45
Sommers Township
Nita City, Nita   99994
(606) 826-9406

Potter v. Shrackle Case File

Exhibit 25

WEATHER BUREAU REPORT
Nita City Weather Bureau

For November 30, 2001

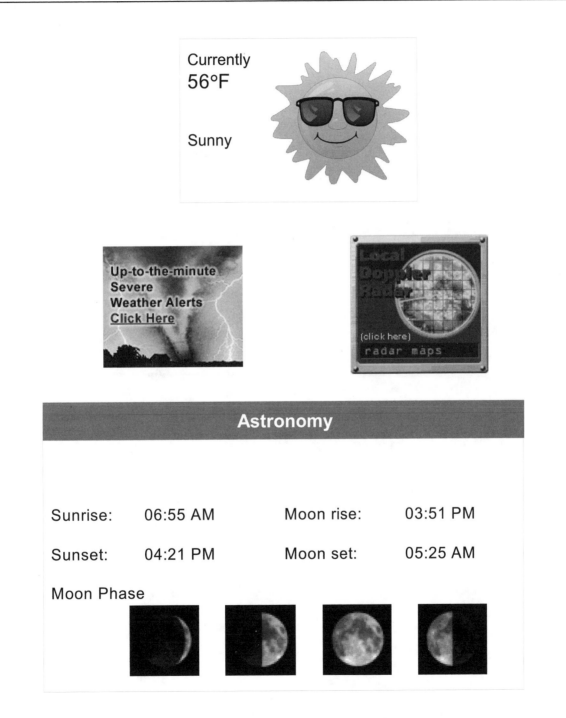

Currently
56°F

Sunny

Up-to-the-minute
Severe
Weather Alerts
Click Here

Local
Doppler
Radar

(click here)
radar maps

Astronomy

Sunrise:	06:55 AM	Moon rise:	03:51 PM
Sunset:	04:21 PM	Moon set:	05:25 AM

Moon Phase

Exhibit 26

NITA MEMORIAL HOSPITAL STATEMENT

NMH Nita Memorial Hospital

444 Medway Park Circle Nita City, Nita 40088   (606) 555-4444

SF-1 Statement
Please note: This is a short form statement listing general charges.
Itemization statements are available upon request for all services and goods provided.

Statement date:	12/7/01
Patient:	Katherine Potter (deceased)
Patient ID:	4478-622-00
Admitted:	Yes
Time/date of initial treatment:	4:18 P.M., 11/30/01
ER attending physician:	Ashley P. Smith, M.D. #609
other physician(s):	Kevin M. Patterson, M.D. #711
Brief description:	Severe head trauma; brain injury and fractured skull result of being struck by moving vehicle. Intermittent consciousness; surgery to relieve pressure on brain
Release date:	TOD 12/4/2001, 4 P.M.

11/30/01	NCH ambulance run service	$840
11/30/01	Emergency room	$4,500
	ER physician (Ref: Ashley P. Smith, M.D. #609)	$4,080
	Medications administered	$1,660
11/30/01-12/4/2001	Intensive care private room and attendant care	
	5 days @ $17,000	$84,200
	Physician, surgery 12/1/02 medications; tests; blood, IV	$11,720
12/4/2001	NCH morgue service	$800
	Total: $107,800	

This statement is for general billing information only and not intended for insurance submission. Insurance claims may be pending and are not necessarily reflected on this statement. Itemizations of all charges are available upon request.

Exhibit 27

ODELL FUNERAL HOME INVOICE

Odell Funeral Home
2002 Eternity Way, Nita City, Nita (606) 555-7734

Confidential Invoice

INVOICE DATE: January 12, 2001

SERVICES FOR: *Katherine Potter, December 11, 2001*

20-gauge reinforced steel "Norabella" casket, sealed	$	8,000.
heavy duty gasket, screw lock, seal kit		229.
delivery included		
General prep services		600.
additional prep		200.
Silk flower casket spray (blue, white, gold)		200.
Memorial stone		2,300.
photo etched		375.
"Restful Garden" Mausoleum, unit 40		3,000.
Peace Garden Cemetery, Nita City, service fee		980.
Limousine 2 hours @ 270.50/hour		541.
10-inch obituary in Nita Journal-Gazette with photo		75.

TOTAL DUE, NET 30: $16,500.00

Established 1924

Exhibit 28

POTTER LETTER TO DR. STEVENS

4920 Thorndale Avenue
Nita City, Nita   99993
September 2, 2001

Dr. Andrew Stevens
Stevens Counseling
1225 North Street
Lisle, Nita   99980

Dear Dr. Stevens:

I am sorry that payment for our last three sessions is late. I guess it goes without saying that Katherine and I don't see eye to eye on the need for this counseling, and it is very difficult for me to get her to even speak calmly about it, much less agree for us to pay for it. Nonetheless, I am enclosing our check in the amount of $300.

I am sorry that we can't continue with you. I thought your advice was very helpful and I appreciated the opportunity to talk with you about the problems that we have been having. I especially want to thank you for your concern about the early retirement issue. Even though Katherine loves her career, I am confident she would like the leisurely life of a college professor's wife even more. When we first got married, I was unable to talk her into having children. She was too career-driven. I hope that I can make more headway on the retirement issue.

Your comments at the last session that it was obvious to you that Katherine and I loved each other very much and would come out of this stronger than ever, make me smile and look forward to the future. I am sure that you are right. Perhaps when we have more time and her career isn't so hectic, I'll be able to persuade Katherine to come back with me to talk to you about the rest of our problems, which don't seem quite so important now. Despite all of the difficulties, I believe that our marriage will work. If it doesn't, so be it. If we can't resolve things, I can leave the marriage and seek a relationship that fulfills my needs.

In any event, keep your fingers crossed for us, please.

Sincerely yours,

Jeffrey T. Potter

Jeffrey T. Potter

Exhibit 29

NITA TRAVEL ETICKET FOR POTTER

NITA TRAVEL COMPANY

eTICKET RECEIPT

Reservation Code:	WQMFKA	Issuing Agent:	Nita City, Nita
Ticket Number:	8675309502425	Issuing Agent:	3BA78/4076
Issuing Airline:	CARRIBEAN AIRLINES	IATA number:	66397478
Date Issued:	30May02	Invoice number:	483228
Customer Number:	8972509574		
Passenger:	TRAVELER/JEFFREY POTTER		

14JUN02	Carribean Air CA 1066	Seat 15B	
From: Nita City, Nita (Nita City Intern'l)		Departs: 730A	Business Confirmed
To: Fort de France, Martinique (FDF)		Arrives: 355P	Fare Basis: TC8BX
			Not Valid Before: 14JUN
			Not Valid After: 14JUN
19JUN02	Carribean Air CA 3631		
From: Fort de France, Martinique (FDF)		Departs: 1150A	Business Confirmed
To: Nita City, Nita (Nita City Intern'l)		Arrives: 820P	Fare Basis: TC8BX
			Not Valid Before: 19JUN
			Not Valid After: 19JUN

Form of Payment: Credit Card - Visa - Charged to Jeffrey Potter

Endorsement/Restrictions: Nonref/Change Fee Plus Fare Diff Applies/Valid US Only

Positive Identification Required for Airport Check-In

Carriage and other service provided by the carrier are subject to conditions of carriage, which are hereby incorporated by reference. These conditions may be obtained from the issuing carrier.

Nita Travel Company . . . Your Gateway to Fun in the Sun!

Exhibit 30

NITA TRAVEL ETICKET FOR TOBIAS

NITA TRAVEL COMPANY   eTICKET RECEIPT

Reservation Code: WQMFKA   Issuing Agent: Nita City, Nita
Ticket Number: 5996739313271   Issuing Agent: 3BA78/4076
Issuing Airline: CARRIBEAN AIRLINES IATA number: 66397478
Date Issued: 30May02   Invoice number: 483228
Customer Number: 2896768575
Passenger: TRAVELER/CHERYL TOBIAS

14JUN02	Carribean Air CA 1066	Seat 15A	
From: Nita City, Nita (Nita City Intern'l)		Departs: 730A	Business Confirmed
To: Fort de France, Martinique (FDF)		Arrives: 355P	Fare Basis: TC8BX
			Not Valid Before: 14JUN
			Not Valid After: 14JUN
19JUN02	Carribean Air CA 3631		
From: Fort de France, Martinique (FDF)		Departs: 1150A	Business Confirmed
To: Nita City, Nita (Nita City Intern'l)		Arrives: 820P	Fare Basis: TC8BX
			Not Valid Before: 19JUN
			Not Valid After: 19JUN

Form of Payment: Credit Card - Visa - Charged to Jeffrey Potter

Endorsement/Restrictions: Nonref/Change Fee Plus Fare Diff Applies/Valid US Only

Positive Identification Required for Airport Check-In

Carriage and other service provided by the carrier are subject to conditions of carriage, which are hereby incorporated by reference. These conditions may be obtained from the issuing carrier.

Nita Travel Company . . . Your Gateway to Fun in the Sun!

Exhibit 31

MARTINIQUE PRINCESS HOTEL BILL

Martinique Princess Hotel
76 Rue de la Plage
Forte de France, Martinique

Name: Mr. & Mrs. Jeffrey Potter   *Guests:* 2

Address: 4920 Thorndale Avenue   *Room:* 1370

      Nita City, Nita

Arrival: 6/14/02   *Departure:* 6/19/02

Date	Description	ID	Ref. No.	Charges	Credits	Balance
6/14/02	Room/Deluxe Suite	MRC	1370	325.00		
6/14/02	I. Room Tax	MIT	1370	29.65		
6/14/02	City Occup. Tax	MOE	1370	10.98		
6/14/02	Room Service	MCH	1370	48.19		
6/15/02	Room/Deluxe Suite	MRC	1370	325.00		
6/15/02	I. Room Tax	MIT	1370	29.65		
6/15/02	City Occup. Tax	MOE	1370	10.98		
6/15/02	Masseuse	MAS	1370	80.50		
6/15/02	Masseuse	MAS	1370	80.50		
6/15/02	Room Service	MCH	1370	28.99		
6/15/02	Room Service	MCH	1370	158.90		
6/16/02	Room/Deluxe Suite	MRC	1370	325.00		
6/16/02	I. Room Tax	MIT	1370	29.65		
6/16/02	City Occup. Tax	MOE	1370	10.98		
6/16/02	Day Spa	MSG	1370	125.29		
6/16/02	Day Spa	MSG	1370	60.13		
6/16/02	Room Service	MCH	1370	33.48		
6/16/02	Laundry Services	MLS	1370	71.17		
6/16/02	Boutique	MBB	1370	148.75		
6/16/02	Room Service	MCH	1370	48.30		
6/16/02	Champagne Cruise	MCC	1370	198.45		
6/1/6/02	Champagne Cruise	MCC	1370	198.45		
6/17/02	Room/Deluxe Suite	MRC	1370	325.00		
6/17/02	I. Room Tax	MIT	1370	29.65		
6/17/02	City Occup. Tax	MOE	1370	10.98		
6/17/02	Room Service	MCH	1370	68.90		
6/17/02	Tarot Card Reader	MTR	1370	51.50		
6/17/02	Masseuse	MAS	1370	80.50		
6/17/02	Room Service	MCH	1370	62.99		
6/17/02	Day Spa	MSG	1370	75.22		
6/17/02	Flower Show	MFB	1370	31.00		
6/17/02	Room Service	MCH	1370	79.42		
6/17/02	Room Service	MCH	1370	108.14		
6/17/02	Movies	MOV	1370	15.00		

Date	Description	ID	Ref. No.	Charges	Credits	Balance
6/18/02	Room/Deluxe Suite	MRC	1370	325.00		
6/18/02	I. Room Tax	MIT	1370	29.65		
6/18/02	City Occup. Tax	MOE	1370	10.98		
6/18/02	Day Spa	MSG	1370	28.68		
6/18/02	Room Service	MCH	1370	43.10		
6/18/02	Island Tour	MCL	1370	58.33		
6/18/02	Island Tour	MCL	1370	58.33		
6/18/02	Room Service	MCH	1370	61.30		
6/18/02	Champagne Cruise	MCC	1370	198.45		
6/18/02	Champagne Cruise	MCC	1370	198.45		
6/19/02	Room Service	MCH	1370	38.95		
Balance						$4,304.52

I agree that my liability for this bill is not waived and agree to be held personally liable in the event that the indicated person, company, or association fails to pay for any part or the full amount of these charges.

Thank you for being our guest at the Martinique Princess Hotel

Exhibit 32

POTTER AND TOBIAS IN MARTINIQUE

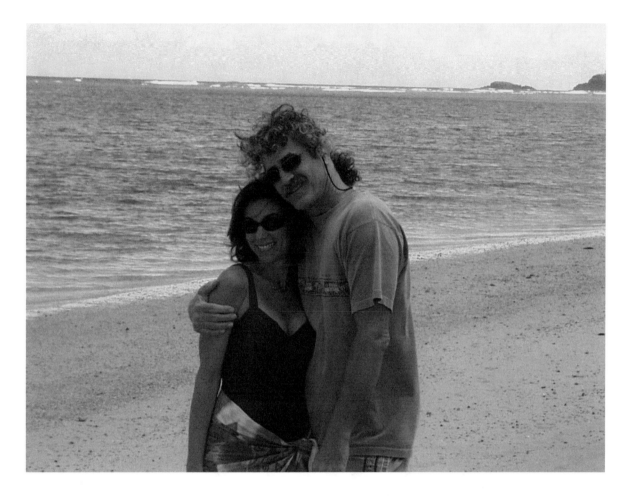

MADDEN & JAMES

Suite 720 • Nita Bank Building • Nita City, Nita 99994 • (721) 555-0003

William James
as attorney for plaintiff to James Barber
at Pierece, Johnson & Clark
Nita National Bank Plaza, Nita City, Nita 99994

March 15, 2003

Re: *Potter v. Shrackle and Shrackle Construction Co.*

Jim:

Although I think there is no obligation to do this under the Rules, I thought I would update Jeffrey Potter's answers at his deposition with regard to his relationship with Cheryl Tobias.

If asked about that relationship at this point, Mr. Potter would state:

> I began a relationship with Cheryl Tobias in the late Spring of 2002. That relationship ended in January 2003.The basis for ending the relationship was that I was unable to move on to another long-term relationship after the death of my wife. Cheryl and I agreed it would be better to break off the relationship at that point.

I would be happy to sign a request to admit to this effect.

Sincerely,

William James

Blank Slide **Slide 1**

Exhibit 1 **Slide 2**

Exhibit 1 **Slide 3**

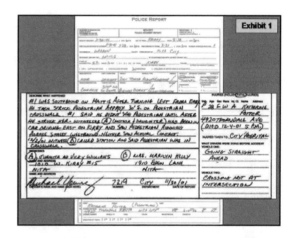

Exhibit 1 **Slide 4**

Exhibit 1 **Slide 5**

Exhibit 1 **Slide 6**

Exhibit 2   **Slide 7**

Exhibit 2a   **Slide 8**

Exhibit 2b   **Slide 9**

Exhibit 2c   **Slide 10**

Exhibit 2d   **Slide 11**

Exhibit 3   **Slide 12**

Exhibit 3a   **Slide 13**

Exhibit 3b   **Slide 14**

Exhibit 3c   **Slide** 15

Exhibit 3d   **Slide 16**

Exhibit 3e   **Slide 17**

Exhibit 4   **Slide 18**

Exhibit 5   **Slide 19**

Exhibit 6   **Slide 20**

Exhibit 7   **Slide 21**

Exhibit 7a   **Slide 22**

Exhibit 8   **Slide 23**

Exhibit 9   **Slide 24**

Exhibit 9a   **Slide 25**

Exhibit 10   **Slide 26**

Exhibit 10a   **Slide 27**

Exhibit 11   **Slide 28**

Exhibit 11a   **Slide 29**

Exhibit 12   **Slide 30**

Exhibit 12a   **Slide 31**

Exhibit 13   **Slide 32**

Exhibit 13a   **Slide 33**

Exhibit 14   **Slide 34**

Exhibit 14a   **Slide 35**

Exhibit 15   **Slide 36**

Exhibit 15a   **Slide 37**

Exhibit 16   **Slide 38**

Exhibit 16a   **Slide 39**

Exhibit 17   **Slide 40**

Exhibit 17a   **Slide 41**

Exhibit 18   **Slide 42**

Exhibit 18a   **Slide 43**

Exhibit 19   **Slide 44**

Exhibit 19a   **Slide 45**

Exhibit 20   **Slide 46**

Exhibit 20a   **Slide 47**

Exhibit 21   **Slide 48**

Exhibit 21a   **Slide 49**

Exhibit 22   **Slide 50**

Exhibit 22   **Slide 51**

Exhibit 22   **Slide 52**

Exhibit 23   **Slide 53**

Exhibit 23   **Slide 54**

Exhibit 23　　　　**Slide 55**

Exhibit 24　　　　**Slide 56**

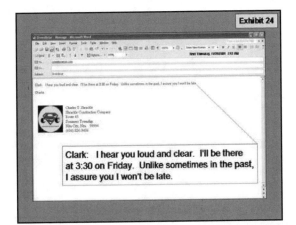

Clark: I hear you loud and clear. I'll be there at 3:30 on Friday. Unlike sometimes in the past, I assure you I won't be late.

Exhibit 24　　　　**Slide 57**

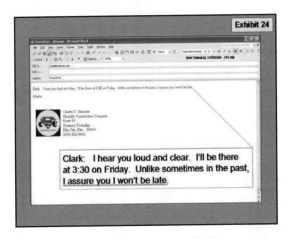

Clark: I hear you loud and clear. I'll be there at 3:30 on Friday. Unlike sometimes in the past, I assure you I won't be late.

Exhibit 24　　　　**Slide 58**

Exhibit 25　　　　**Slide 59**

Exhibit 25　　　　**Slide 60**

Exhibit 26   **Slide 61**

Exhibit 26   **Slide 62**

Exhibit 26   **Slide 63**

Exhibit 26   **Slide 64**

Exhibit 27   **Slide 65**

Exhibit 28   **Slide 66**

Exhibit 28   **Slide 67**

Exhibit 28   **Slide 68**

Exhibit 28   **Slide 69**

Exhibit 29   **Slide 70**

Exhibit 30   **Slide 71**

Exhibit 31   **Slide 72**

Exhibit 31   **Slide 73**

Exhibit 32   **Slide 74**

Exhibit 33   **Slide 75**

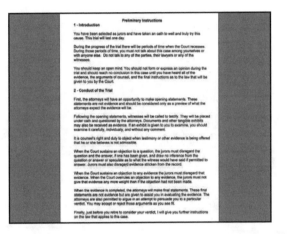

Jury Inst. Prelim.   **Slide 76**

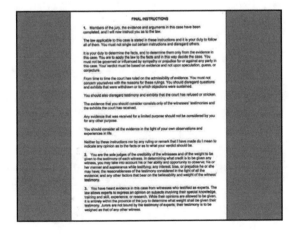

Jury Inst. P. 1   **Slide 77**

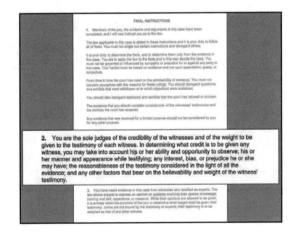

Jury Inst. p. 1   **Slide 78**

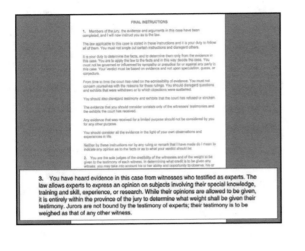

Jury Inst. p.1 **Slide 79**

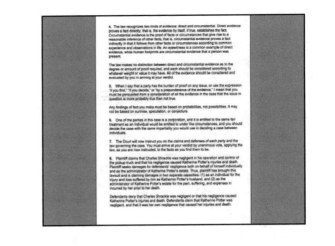

Jury Inst. p. 2 **Slide 80**

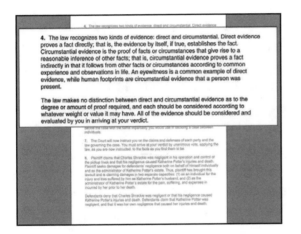

Jury Inst. p. 2 **Slide 81**

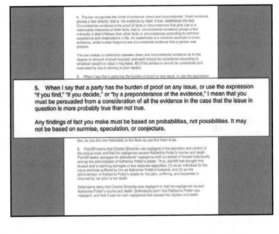

Jury Inst. p. 2 **Slide 82**

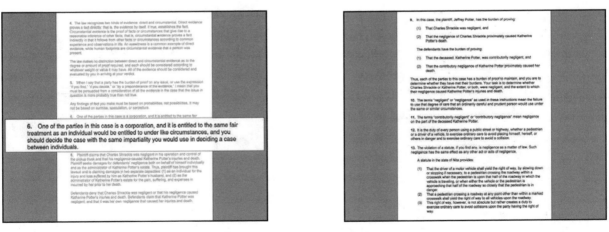

Jury Inst. p.2 **Slide 83**

Jury Inst. p. 3 **Slide 84**

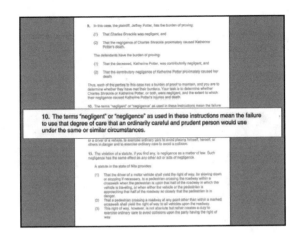

Jury Inst. p. 3   **Slide 85**

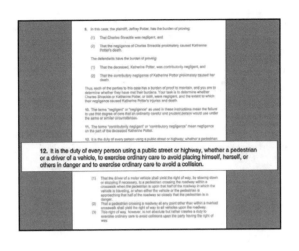

Jury Inst. p. 3   **Slide 86**

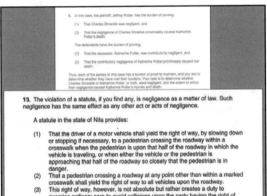

Jury Inst. p. 3   **Slide 87**

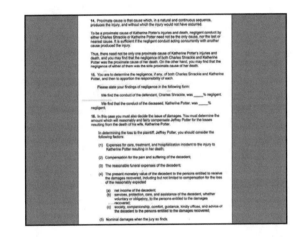

Jury Inst. p. 4   **Slide 88**

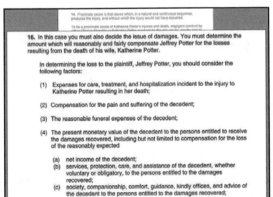

Jury Inst. p. 4   **Slide 89**

Jury Inst. p. 5   **Slide 90**

197
Potter v. Shrackle Case File

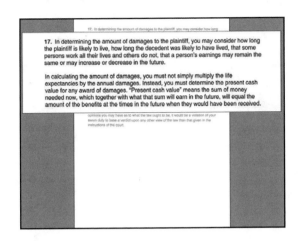

Jury Inst. P. 5   **Slide 91**

Verdict Form   **Slide 92**

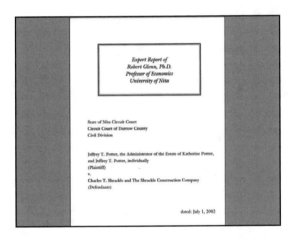

Glenn Report p. 1   **Slide 93**

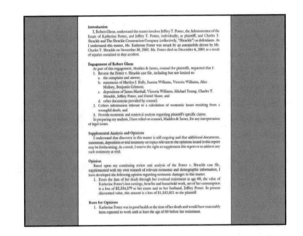

Glenn Report p. 2   **Slide 94**

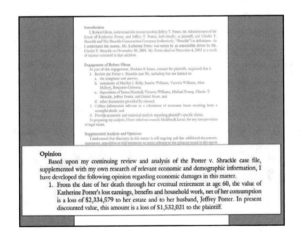

Glenn Report p. 2   **Slide 95**

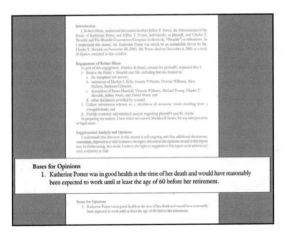

Glenn Report p. 2   **Slide 96**

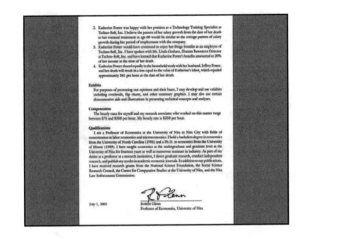

Glenn Report p. 3   **Slide 97**

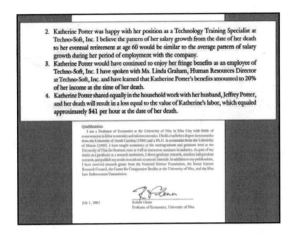

Glenn Report p. 3   **Slide 98**

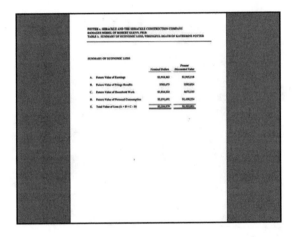

Glenn Table 1   **Slide 99**

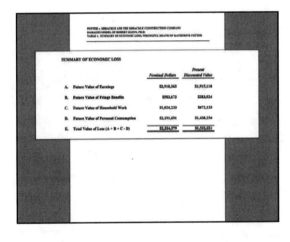

Glenn Table 1   **Slide 100**

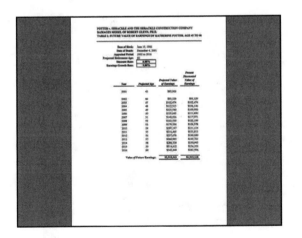

Glenn Table 2   **Slide 101**

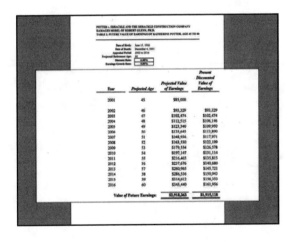

Glenn Table 2   **Slide 102**

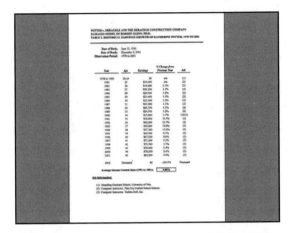

Glenn Table 3 **Slide 103**

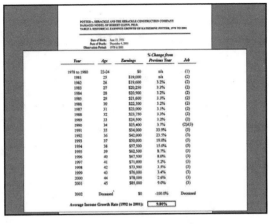

Glenn Table 3 **Slide 104**

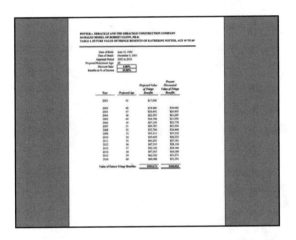

Glenn Table 4 **Slide 105**

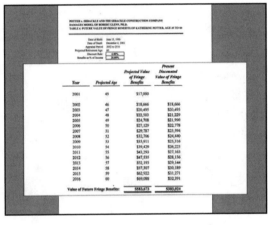

Glenn Table 4 **Slide 106**

Glenn Table 5 **Slide 107**

Glenn Table 5 **Slide 108**

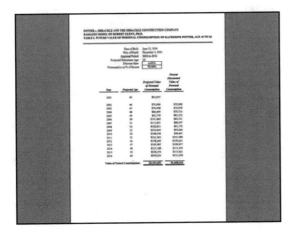

Glenn Table 6   **Slide 109**

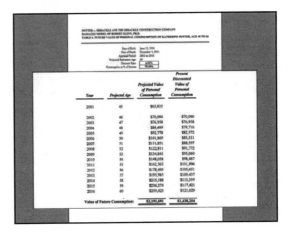

Glenn Table 6   **Slide 110**

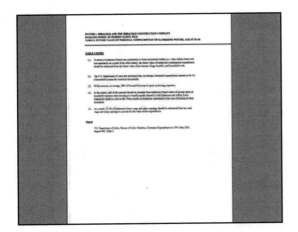

Glenn Table 6 Notes **Slide 111**

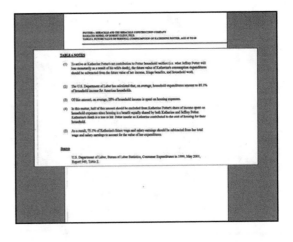

Glenn Table 6 Notes **Slide 112**

Glenn CV   **Slide 113**

Buchanan Report   **Slide 114**

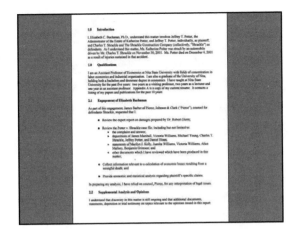

Buchanan Report p. 1 **Slide 115**

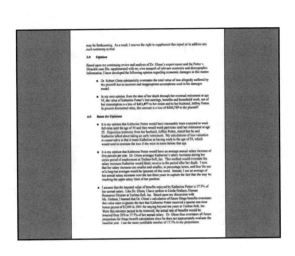

Buchanan Report p. 2 **Slide 116**

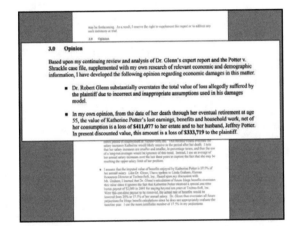

Buchanan Report p. 2 **Slide 117**

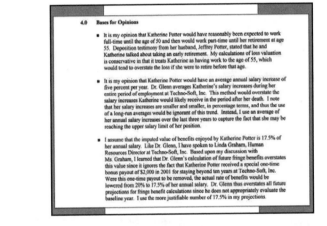

Buchanan Report p. 2 **Slide 118**

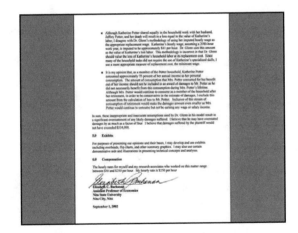

Buchanan Report p. 3 **Slide 119**

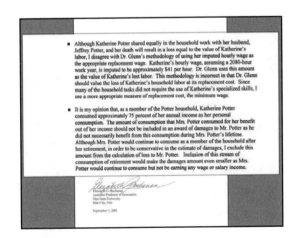

Buchanan Report p. 3 **Slide 120**

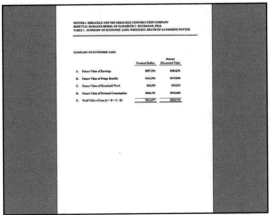

Buchanan Table 1   **Slide 121**

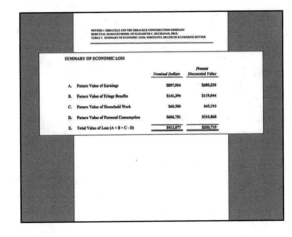

Buchanan Table 1   **Slide 122**

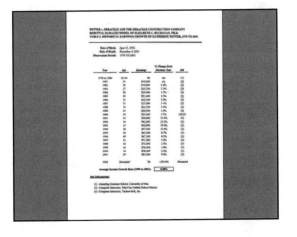

Buchanan Table 2   **Slide 123**

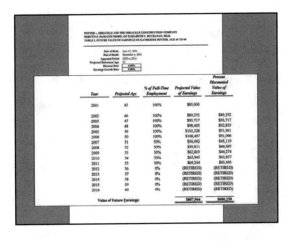

Buchanan Table 2   **Slide 124**

Buchanan Table 3   **Slide 125**

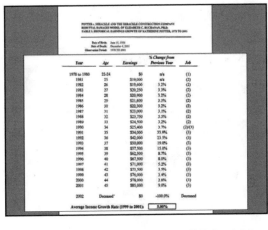

Buchanan Table 3   **Slide 126**

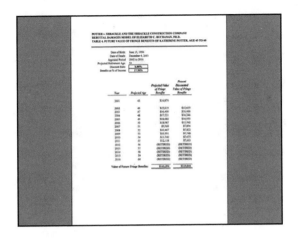

Buchanan Table 4 **Slide 127**

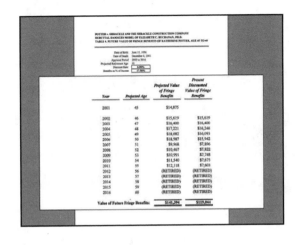

Buchanan Table 4 **Slide 128**

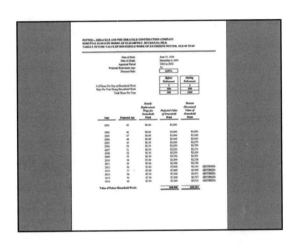

Buchanan Table 5 **Slide 129**

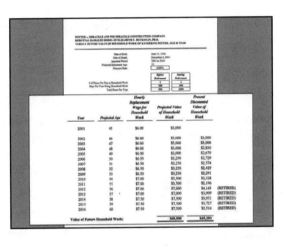

Buchanan Table 5 **Slide 130**

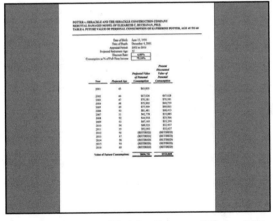

Buchanan Table 6 **Slide 131**

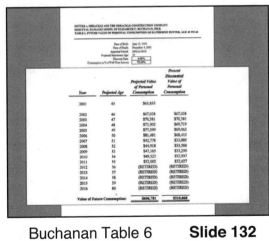

Buchanan Table 6 **Slide 132**

Buchanan CV
Slide 133

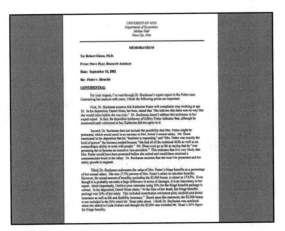

Dyer Memo p. 1
Slide 134

Dyer Memo p. 2
Slide 135

Impeachment Slides
Slide 136

Potter Transcript
Slide 137

Potter Video
Slide 138

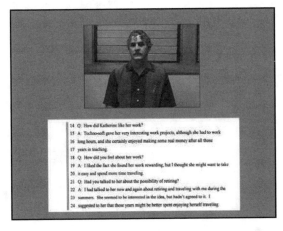

Potter Video
and Transcript

Slide 139

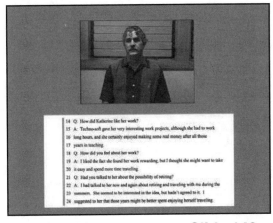

Potter Photo
and Transcript

Slide 140

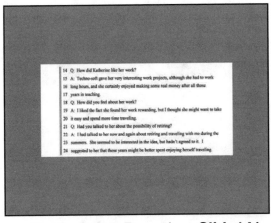

Potter Q & A Reveal

Slide141

Shrackle Transcript

Slide 142

Shrackle Video

Slide 143

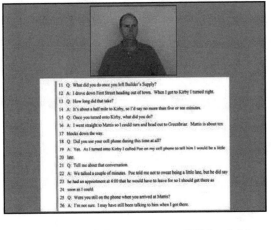

Shrackle Video
and Transcript

Slide 144

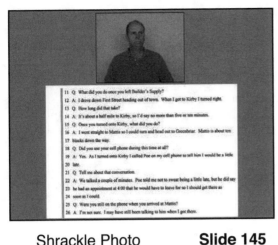

Shrackle Photo
and Transcript   **Slide 145**

Shrackle Q & A Reveal **Slide 146**

Marshall Transcript   **Slide 147**

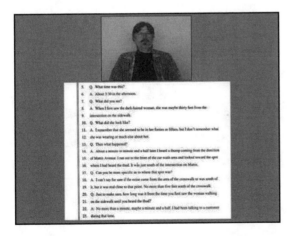

Marshall Video   **Slide 148**

Marshall Video
and Transcript   **Slide 149**

Marshall Photo
and Transcript   **Slide 150**

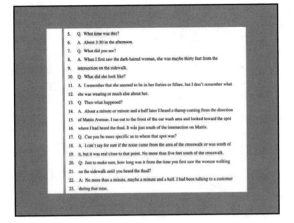

Marshall Q & A Reveal **Slide 151**

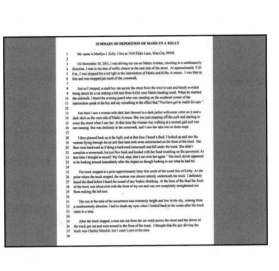

Kelly Depo. p. 1   **Slide 152**

Kelly Depo. p. 1   **Slide 153**

Kelly Depo. p. 1   **Slide 154**

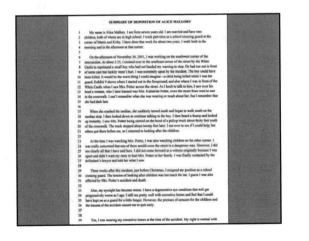

Mallory Depo. p. 1   **Slide 155**

Mallory Depo. p. 1   **Slide 156**

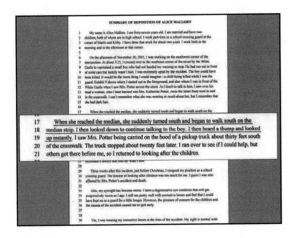

SUMMARY OF DEPOSITION OF ALICE MALLORY

1   My name is Alice Mallory. I am forty-seven years old. I am married and have two
2   children, both of whom are in high school. I work part-time as a school crossing guard at the
3   corner of Mattis and Kirby. I have done that work for about two years. I work both in the
4   morning and in the afternoon at that corner.
5
6   On the afternoon of November 30, 2001, I was working on the southwest corner of the
7   intersection. At about 3:25, I crossed over to the southeast corner of the street by the White
8   Castle to reprimand a small boy who had not heeded my warning to stop. He had run out in front
9   of some cars but luckily wasn't hurt. I was extremely upset by the incident. The boy could have
10 been killed. It would be the worst thing I could imagine—a child being killed while I was the
11 guard. Exhibit 9 shows where I started out in the foreground, and also where I was in front of the
12 White Castle when I saw Mrs. Potter across the street. As I knelt to talk to him, I saw over his
13 head a woman, who I later learned was Mrs. Katherine Potter, cross the street from west to east
14 in the crosswalk. I can't remember what she was wearing or much about her, but I remember that
15 she had dark hair.
16
17 When she reached the median, she suddenly turned south and began to walk south on the

---

17 **When she reached the median, she suddenly turned south and began to walk south on the**
18 **median strip. I then looked down to continue talking to the boy. I then heard a thump and looked**
19 **up instantly. I saw Mrs. Potter being carried on the hood of a pickup truck about thirty feet south**
20 **of the crosswalk. The truck stopped about twenty feet later. I ran over to see if I could help, but**
21 **others got there before me, so I returned to looking after the children.**

---

28 accident's lawyer and me out when I saw.
29
30 Three weeks after this incident, just before Christmas, I resigned my position as a school
31 crossing guard. The tension of looking after children was too much for me. I guess I was also
31 affected by Mrs. Potter's accident and death.
32
33 Also, my eyesight has become worse. I have a degenerative eye condition that will get
34 progressively worse as I age. I still see pretty well with corrective lenses and feel that I could
35 have kept on as a guard for a little longer. However, the pressure of concern for the children and
36 the trauma of the accident caused me to quit early.
37
38
39 Yes, I was wearing my corrective lenses at the time of the accident. My sight is normal with

Mallory Depo. p. 1   **Slide 157**

SPECIAL IMPEACHMENT PROBLEMS

Problems 1, 2, and 3 are designed to be used in conjunction with the special impeachment slides that come with the PowerPoint slide show in order to learn how to integrate technology into the impeachment process. There are several options for display that accompany the transcript segment for each witness: (1) the written Q and A only; (2) the video only; (3) the video with transcript; (4) a photo taken of the deponent with transcript; (5) the Q and A revealing one at a time. For Problem 1 the slides are numbers 146–150; Problem 2, 151–155; Problem 3, 156–160.

Problem 1 – Jeffrey Potter

Assume that Jeffrey Potter is called as a witness for plaintiff and testifies at trial as follows:

"She would hear nothing about retiring. She had no interest in it at all."

(a) **For the defendant, cross-examine Potter based upon his deposition.**

(b) **For the plaintiff, conduct any necessary redirect examination.**

Problem 2 – Charles Shrackle

Assume that Charles Shrackle is called as a witness for defendant and testifies at trial as follows:

Q. What happened after you left Builders Supply?

A. I called Poe just as I was pulling out of Builders Supply. It must have been about ten after three.

Q. Did you use your cell phone at any other time before the accident?

A. No.

(a) **For the plaintiff, cross-examine Shrackle based upon his deposition.**

(b) **For the defendant, conduct any necessary redirect examination.**

Problem 3 – James Marshall

Assume that James Marshall is called as a witness for the plaintiff and testifies as follows:

> Q. How long was it from the time you first saw the woman walking towards the crosswalk until you heard the thud?
>
> A. No more than a couple of seconds, maybe five seconds, certainly no more than ten.

(a) For the defendant, cross-examine Marshall based upon his deposition.

(b) For the defendant, cross-examine Marshall based upon his handwritten statement.

(c) For the plaintiff, conduct any necessary redirect examination.

Problem 4 – Marilyn Kelly

Assume that Marilyn Kelly is called as a witness for the plaintiff and testifies at trial as follows:

> "At the time of the thud the front of the truck was about half-way through the crosswalk. It was not completely straightened out from making the left turn."

(a) For the defendant, cross-examine Kelly based upon her deposition.

(b) For the plaintiff, conduct any necessary redirect examination.

Problem 5 – Alice Mallory

Assume that Alice Mallory is called as a witness for the defendant and testifies at trial as follows:

> "When the woman reached the median, she suddenly turned south and began to walk south on the median strip. She had walked at least 15 or 20 feet south of the crosswalk when I looked down to continue talking to the boy."

(a) For the plaintiff, cross-examine Mallory based upon her deposition.

(b) For the defendant, conduct any necessary redirect examination.

HOW TO USE THE CD

The CD that comes with this case file contains a PowerPoint slide show, along with digital copies of exhibits and video clips for the file. If you want to view the already prepared PowerPoint slide show on the CD, here is what you do:

1. Insert the CD into the CD drive of your computer.

2. For XP users, click on Start, find and double click the "My Computer" icon in the banner that appears. For earlier Windows operating systems, go to the Windows Desktop and double click on the My Computer icon, which looks like this.

3. This displays icons for each of the drives on your computer (usually A, C, D and so on) together with some other basic controls. You are going to use the icon for the CD drive, which looks like this.

   Wait for a few seconds while the computer identifies the CD. It will change to show that it can read the disk by displaying a name next to the icon that says "Potter CD."

4. Double click on this icon. This displays each of the folders on the CD. One is called "Exhibit scans" which holds that digital files of the paper documents in the case. Double click on the folder called "PowerPoint slide show & video clips." This displays the PowerPoint icon, which looks like this.

   Double click to open the slide show, which will come up in normal screen mode. To play the show, hit the F5 key on your keyboard.

The first slide of the presentation will appear. It is a blank slide, black in color.

- To display any other slide in the slide show, simply type the slide number (**NOT** the exhibit number) as shown in the thumbnail printouts at the back of the case file and hit the "Enter" key.

- To see the next slide in order, click the left mouse or press the space bar.

- To go back one slide, press the "Page Up" key or up arrow.

- To go to any other slide, type the slide number and hit the Enter key.

- To play animations (if the slide contains any), either left click the mouse or press the space bar to initiate each animation.

- To take projected images off the screen or monitor and return to a neutral blank screen, type in "1" plus "Enter" or press the "Home" key to return to the first slide in the show, the blank slide.

- To play the video clips, bring up the slide you want by typing the slide number and hitting "Enter," then move the mouse cursor into the image (you might need to move the mouse around rapidly for a second or two to see the cursor on the screen). Once in the video image, the cursor will change from a pointed arrow into a little white hand. That is your signal that the video is ready to play. Left click once and the video will play. You can stop and start the video with a left mouse click so long as the cursor remains inside the image.

TO TRANSFER THE POWERPOINT SHOW TO YOUR COMPUTER'S HARD DRIVE

For best results, it is highly recommended that you download the PowerPoint slide show and accompanying video clips from the CD to your hard drive. The slide shows and video clips will play faster and much more smoothly this way. The easiest way to accomplish this is as follows.

1. Open the CD in My Computer.

2. Right click on the folder "PowerPoint slide show & video clips" and select "Copy," then click "Back" and double click on the "Local Disk" or hard drive (usually "C:"), right click in an open space and select "Paste." The folder will be copied to your hard drive. To create a shortcut on your desktop for quick and easy access to the PowerPoint slide show, open the folder you just copied and pasted by double clicking on it, right click on the PowerPoint slide show, put the cursor over "Sent To" and select "Desktop (create shortcut)."

3. If the video clips do not play within the PowerPoint slide as it initially comes up in the PowerPoint presentation mode, but instead become enlarged, click on "Start," "Control Panel," "Display," "Settings," "Advanced," "Troubleshoot," tab, and under Hardware Acceleration move the slide from "Full" to "None" to fix it.

To answer other questions you may have, please refer to *PowerPoint for Litigators*, Siemer, Rothschild, Stein, and Solomon (NITA, 2000) or *PowerPoint 2002 for Litigators*, Siemer, Rothschild (NITA 2003).

NOTE REGARDING EXHIBITS

To access case file exhibits 1–32 on the accompanying CD, please open the PowerPoint slide show, which can be found in the folder labeled "PowerPoint slides and video clip."

While most of these exhibits can also be found in the folder labeled "Exhibit scans," a few of the documents are not included in this folder. Please rest assured, however, that every document you may need is contained on the CD.